The Only Business Writing Book
You'll Ever Need

Also by Laura Brown

How to Write Anything

The
Only
Business
Writing Book
You'll
Ever Need

Laura Brown

Foreword by Rich Karlgaard

W. W. NORTON & COMPANY
Independent Publishers Since 1923
New York | London

For information about permission to reproduce selections from this book, write to Permissions, W. W. Norton & Company, Inc., 500 Fifth Avenue, New York, NY 10110

For information about special discounts for bulk purchases, please contact W. W. Norton Special Sales at specialsales@wwnorton.com or 800-233-4830

Manufacturing by LSC Communications Harrisonburg
Book design by Lovedog Studio
Production manager: Julia Druskin

Library of Congress Cataloging-in-Publication Data

Names: Brown, Laura, 1959– author.
Title: The only business writing book you'll ever need / Laura Brown ; foreword by Rich Karlgaard.
Description: First Edition. | New York : W. W. Norton & Company, [2019] | Includes index.
Identifiers: LCCN 2018046418 | ISBN 9780393635324 (hardcover)
Subjects: LCSH: Business writing.
Classification: LCC HF5718.3 .B765 2019 | DDC 808.06/665—dc23
LC record available at https://lccn.loc.gov/2018046418

W. W. Norton & Company, Inc., 500 Fifth Avenue, New York, N.Y. 10110
www.wwnorton.com

W. W. Norton & Company Ltd., 15 Carlisle Street, London W1D 3BS

1 2 3 4 5 6 7 8 9 0

This book is dedicated to my teacher
Catherine M. Rose

Contents

Foreword

I fell in love with snappy writing in high school, and no thanks to my English literature classes. Credit goes to a birthday gift of a *Sports Illustrated* subscription. Back in the 1970s and 1980s, *SI* magazine had a stable of top sportswriters, among them Dan Jenkins (college football and golf), Anita Verschoth (Olympic sports), and Frank Deford, in my opinion the best profile writer of the last fifty years.

I always wondered why these writers, and others of my favorites, were able to do what they did. Why was Tom Wolfe's *The Right Stuff* so gripping that the reader felt physically propelled like the astronauts? Why was dialogue so true in the novels of Elmore Leonard, Carl Hiaasen, and John Sandford?

Later I had the privilege of working with Tom Wolfe. While the editor of a futurist magazine, *Forbes ASAP*, I assigned Wolfe a five-hundred-word piece on the 1990s Internet bubble. He agreed to write it, and then weeks later, on a Saturday, I happened to be standing by the office fax machine. (Remember those?) The fax started its hiss and screech, then spat out fifty-eight pages of triple-spaced copy evidently written on a typewriter. It was Wolfe's draft, and it was nine thousand words long.

Why triple-spaced? I would soon find out.

During the next few weeks, Wolfe sent revisions to his triple-spaced draft. Some of his revisions were typewritten and looked to be Scotch-taped over the original text. Other revisions were handwritten and appeared as exclamation points and even, oddly, musical notes.

What I learned through the Tom Wolfe project was that Wolfe was a very good first-draft writer. No surprise there. But he became Tom Wolfe as we knew him, with his singular and unparalleled prose style, only through revision. And the revision was about craft. Tom Wolfe, great American prose stylist, was a master craftsman.

The *craft* of writing is wildly underappreciated. Many people mistakenly think great writing is a product of talent, but I'd say it's one-third talent, two-thirds craft. The three jobs of any writer are to be read, understood, and remembered. Smart craft alone is enough to accomplish the first two. Whether you'll be remembered is a matter of your talent, passion, and point of view. But if your craft is poor and you write gummed-up sentences and incoherent paragraphs, no one but your cat will care about your passion and POV.

To anyone who wants to be readable, understandable, and memorable in their writing I recommend a few classics, such as Stephen King's *On Writing: A Memoir of the Craft* and George Orwell's *Why I Write*. These will disabuse you of the temptation to ever be dull, obtuse, wishy-washy, or clichéd again. Another useful exercise is to retype favorite passages from your favorite writers. That and just write—a lot. Bank those ten thousand hours. Such practice will earn you a bachelor's degree in the craft of writing.

But you can't stop there, because now it's time to get your MBA in prose. For that I enthusiastically recommend Laura Brown's *The Only Business Writing Book You'll Ever Need*. Lord, does the world need Laura's book! If you think the need for clear, crisp writing is outdated, you're not paying attention. The richest person in the world, Jeff Bezos of Amazon, begins his staff meetings with everyone silently reading the Bezos-assigned memo of the day. Would you like to be the writer of that memo? You think you might be under a wee bit of pressure to make yourself clear, credible, and persuasive? Ya think?

As Laura perceptively notes, all business writing is an "ask" of some kind. Your ask is a meeting, a sale, money to hire someone, or legal help to justify a sacking. All business writing, whether text, e-mail, or memo, is an ask. Your success in business is predicated upon getting people to say yes to your asks. Business writing, you see, is high-stakes writing.

Go ahead. Be muddled, obtuse, and clichéd in your business writing if you want. I can almost guarantee you won't get anywhere useful. Learn to write right, and start with this book.

Rich Karlgaard
Publisher and futurist, Forbes Media
Author, *Late Bloomers: The Power of Patience in a World Obsessed with Early Achievement*

Preface

Over the past thirty years, my clients have often asked me to recommend a good book about business writing. My first book, *How to Write Anything*, is nearly six hundred pages long and contains a lot of information about writing for school and writing in your personal life, so it's not the kind of handbook my clients were looking for. I haven't been able to find another business writing book I would recommend wholeheartedly, so I've written my own.

Most business writing books on the market are too long, too academic, and out-of-date. Many of them still treat e-mail as a newfangled thing. Many of them sound like they were written by English professors rather than by people who work in an office.

Business writing has changed tremendously over the past few decades, and it continues to change rapidly. At the same time, writing is becoming more important in business. We're all writing more at work than ever before. The advent of the Internet, with the explosion of e-mail and mobile communication, coupled with globalization and virtual teaming, means that writing is the primary form of communication in many work settings. If you can't write well, your chances for success are limited.

After thirty years of training and coaching business writers, I felt pretty confident that I knew what kind of help they needed. To be sure, though, I conducted a ten-question online survey on business writing, asking respondents what they write at work, where they have the most trouble writing at work, where they think their colleagues could use the most help with their writing, and whether they would find a new business writing book helpful. The survey was launched in April 2016 among my clients and associates; was promoted on Facebook, Twitter, and LinkedIn; and ended up with 528 responses. (See Appendix A for the list of survey questions.) The responses proved invaluable in helping me create a book that responds to the needs of today's business writers.

I hope this book will make writing at work a lot easier for you. If you have any feedback, I'd love to hear it. Please write to me at laura@ howtowriteanything.com.

Introduction

The aim of this book is to help you get all of your writing done faster and to build your confidence and skills as a business writer. In the pages that follow, you'll find:

* A **seven-step method** you can use with all kinds of business writing

You can apply these seven steps to anything you write at work, and you can do so *quickly*. You'll find before and after examples of what happens when you apply the step to a sample piece of writing. I've put the steps together in a checklist you can use as you write at work.

You'll notice that you're already good at some of these steps and less good at others. Feel free to spend as much or as little time with each step as you like. The last thing I want is for you to have to read the whole book to learn a system. Instead, the book is designed for you to pick it up and find helpful tips you can use right away.

* Guidance on the **most popular types of business writing**, including e-mails, instant messages, and PowerPoint presentations

You'll find detailed advice on how to write these successfully, as well as special tips on how to implement the seven steps in the various kinds of documents you write.

⁂ Easy-to-use **resources** on writing skills, style, grammar, and punctuation

Are you looking for a remedy for writer's block? Don't remember exactly when to use a comma? Can't recall what the heck a semicolon is for? Always confusing "affect" and "effect"? You'll get this information and more in the "Resources" chapter.

You'll also find brief sections to help you with things like tone, structure, formatting, and writing for mobile devices.

Finally, you'll find sidebars written by a group of experts in various fields, offering their insights and tried-and-true methods for writing successfully in business.

Throughout the book, the emphasis is on practical application in a real business setting. It's my hope that this book will answer your questions, clear some blocks, and get you writing quickly and efficiently at work.

FOR INSTRUCTORS AND STUDENTS

For instructors who wish to use this book in writing courses, additional resources are available on my website at www.howtowriteanything. com. Students will find downloadable samples of different genres of business writing, as well as other writing resources, there

HOW TO WRITE ANYTHING

Readers who are interested in writing guidance that goes beyond business writing should have a look at my previous book, *How to Write Anything: A Complete Guide* (W. W. Norton, 2014). With nearly six hundred pages of guidance, *How to Write Anything* combines a unique approach to writing with a comprehensive encyclopedia of more than two hundred writing tasks—complete with model outlines, dos and don'ts, and examples—designed to help you get through all of life's writing tasks.

The section on writing in your personal life includes useful tips spanning thank-you notes, apologies, wedding invitations, notes to teachers, condolence messages, and obituaries. The section on writing at school covers the basics of note taking and bibliographies, the compare/contrast essay, lab reports, and school newspaper articles. It also offers tips on written communications for the academic environment, such as e-mails requesting a recommendation from a teacher or professor.

You can learn more about the book and download free excerpts from my website at www.howtowriteanything.com.

To Write or
Not to Write?

*"Someone should write about how technology writing
has ruined relationships. Sometimes e-mail is misused,
misunderstood. The misuse of e-mail and other technology
has made me start picking up the phone again, calling
people, and setting up face-to-face meetings."*

—SURVEY RESPONDENT

Before we get started, I'd like to point out that writing isn't always the best way to communicate in business. Writing, even good writing, can slow down communication and decision-making. Imperfect writing can create misunderstandings. Thoughtless writing can breach confidentiality and expose you and your organization to risk. Before you write, you're wise to consider if writing is the best communication option in your particular case.

This flowchart can help you think about whether your message might be conveyed better through a phone call or a face-to-face conversation than through a written communication. The flowchart isn't meant to be exhaustive; there are other situations where a face-to-face conversation might be better than a written message—for instance, when you need to apologize for something. But it's a good starting place to help you decide to write . . . or not to write.

To Write or Not to Write

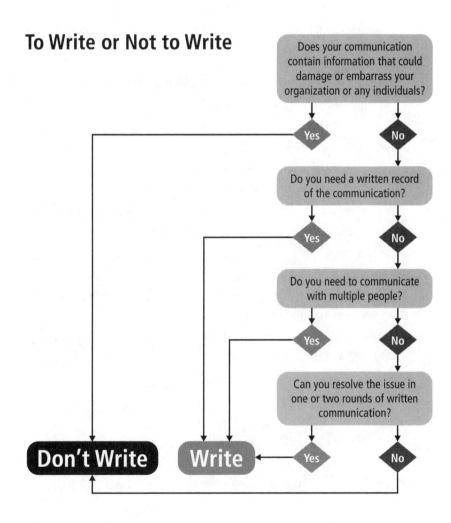

What Communications Professionals Want You to Know About Writing at Work

Anita Gupta

Creating a paper trail at work—making sure there's a written record of discussions and decisions—can be useful, but it can also create a risk for yourself and your organization. The news is full of stories about business e-mails—either leaked or uncovered as part of a legal investigation—that reveal misconduct or cast the organization in an unsavory light. Communications professionals know that a little caution with the written word could have saved these writers and their organizations from bad publicity, regulatory action, or legal action—and we want you to exercise the same caution.

Applying a simple test to everything you write at work can help protect your organization from serious consequences. Ask yourself, "How would I feel if my boss read what I've written?" and "How would I feel if my message ended up on the front page of the *New York Times*?" If the answers to those questions make you even a little uncomfortable, delete what you've written. Consider conveying the message in person, or not conveying it at all.

The catalog of risky content is quite broad, including anything illegal or unethical, anything that even *appears to be* illegal or unethical, and generally anything that might make your organization look bad. Sexist or racist remarks, jokes about misusing expense accounts, jokes about overbilling, and comments that insult your colleagues, clients, or customers—all of these can get your organization in trouble.

It's also worth remembering that in protecting your organization, you're protecting yourself, too. The e-mails, texts, and instant messages that you write at work are the property of your company, and your company can review them at any time, without your knowledge or consent. If your messages show that you're violating legal or ethical standards or company policies, you can be dismissed.

With the advent of social media, the category of "writing at work" extends further than it used to. Even though you don't explicitly represent your organization when you post on social media sites, remember that anything you post can reflect on your company. When you post on social media, give some thought to what your boss might think. Large organizations with legal and risk management departments usually issue guidelines about personal use of social media and tend to be the most sensitive about what their employees do, but all companies care what you do online. It might not seem fair, but no matter who you work for, you can lose your job for behaving badly on social media. Things like advocating violence, using excessive profanity, posting pornography, or using abusive language on social media can show your organization in a bad light and can put your job in jeopardy.

Remembering that your messages at work aren't private and exercising a little common sense can help protect you and your organization from the potentially risky consequences of putting it in writing.

Anita Gupta is head of global media relations and regional head of corporate communications and responsibility, Americas at Deutsche Post DHL Group.

What Kind of Writer Are You?

In thirty years as a writing coach and trainer, I've seen all kinds of writers. There are many ways to approach a writing task, and none of them is the *only* right way. What's important is for you to understand which approach works best for you and to use that approach, not to try to force yourself to work in a way that someone else has dictated.

As I see it, most writers are either **planners** or **editors**.

Planners like to map things out before they start to write. They organize their content; they make outlines. Editors, on the other hand, tend to jump in and write, and then go back and revise later. Of course, most people do a little of both—you pretty much have to—but most people have a preferred approach. I'm an editor myself; I tend to write a draft and go back and fix it up later. It took me years to accept that it was all right for me to work this way, that I wasn't a miserable failure because I don't outline. It's also all right for *you* to use whichever approach you like best.

In the seven steps that follow, you'll see guidance useful for all kinds of writers, and you'll also see guidance specifically for planners and for editors, so that you can make the most of your preferred approach to writing.

If you've never thought about this idea before, or if you're not sure exactly how you prefer to work, it's worth giving it some thought. The more self-aware you become as a writer, the more success you'll have in getting your writing done quickly, efficiently, and effectively.

The Seven Steps

In this section, we'll explore a seven-step process that you can use to write anything you need to write. You've probably seen lists like the one on page 10 before. There are lots of sensible ways to organize and describe the writing process. This one is distilled from my thirty years of work as a writing coach and trainer, and I think it's comprehensive. If you follow it, you'll get your writing done. Feel free to adapt it and tailor it to your own needs.

As you browse through these steps, you'll see that they work together; once you get the hang of one, you'll probably find yourself unconsciously addressing the others. For example, once you have clarity on Step 1, *Get the ask clear*, you might find that your openings automatically get *stronger and more specific* (Step 3). When you really think about *writing for your reader* (Step 2), you'll choose your *content* in a more targeted way (Step 5).

The ultimate point of this process is not to train you to follow a step-by-step process slavishly for the rest of your life, but to make you a better and faster writer. Working with the steps is a means to that end. You should feel free to use the steps any way you want. You can try working with them in numerical order, or you can browse around and pick up tips here and there. Keep what's useful to you; discard what isn't. Using the steps will help you refine your own writing process and become a stronger and more confident writer.

THE SEVEN STEPS . . .

. . . to Success with Everything You Write at Work

1 **Get the Ask Clear**

Make sure you know why you're writing and what you're trying to achieve.

2 **Write for Your Reader**

Focus on what your reader needs and expects, not just on what you want. Make your writing appeal to your reader.

3 **Start Strong and Specific**

Craft an opening that makes your purpose clear and motivates your reader to keep reading.

4 **Be Concise**

Make your point as efficiently as possible.

5 **Fill In Missing Content; Delete Extraneous Content**

Do a quick content check to ensure that your readers are getting what they and nothing they don't need.

6 **Write in Plain English**

Business jargon can creep in unnoticed. Distinguish yourself by saying what you mean in plain English.

7 **If Something Feels Wrong, Fix It**

If you feel like there's something wrong with what you've just drafted, there probably is. Instead of sending something you feel uncomfortable with, take a minute to figure out what's wrong, and fix it.

STEP 1: GET THE ASK CLEAR

*"If you want me to respond to your e-mail, you HAVE to
let me know exactly what you want, and you have to do it
fast. I don't have time to guess what I'm supposed to do."*

—SURVEY RESPONDENT

Whenever you write, you're asking for something from your reader. It might be a direct request—"please do this," "please send me that." It might also be a simple request for the reader's attention, in which case the ask is really "please read this information and take it in."

The ask might be quick, or it might be extended over many pages; one sort of longer ask is a business plan, where the entire document is an argument in support of the request "please invest money in our venture." It might be an initial e-mail intended to open a discussion—for instance, about changing procedures or hiring a new staff member.

The ask also might be an *implicit* ask, as when a company publishes a white paper on research it has conducted or a process it has developed. The white paper doesn't explicitly request that the reader hire the firm, but if it's well done it appeals to a need the reader has and piques his interest in learning more. In business, there's an implicit ask embedded in most knowledge sharing and thought leadership.

Whether you're asking your reader to take action now, to start thinking about taking action in the future, or just to pay attention, your communication will be more effective if she understands why you're writing—if you can **get the ask clear**.

Getting the ask clear depends on getting clarity in your own mind about what you really want from the reader. Getting the ask clear in your own head isn't always as easy as it sounds. How many times have you read one of those meandering e-mails and wondered, *"What exactly do you want from me?"* Maybe you've even reread one of your own e-mails after you've sent it and cringed a little bit at how unclear it seems in retrospect.

Just for a moment, entertain the idea that you're not entirely sure what you want, or at least you're not as clear as you ought to be. It happens more often than you think.

Let's take a look at a couple of examples.

Luc's company is getting ready to sign a three-year contract with SARCO. The evening after the team's most recent call with SARCO, some things are bothering Luc, so he sends this e-mail to his team:

> I have concerns about the latest draft of the contract with SARCO. We talked about this on the call, but I'm still not sure what the sign-off process is. And the requirements for Year 3 are vague— if they want something different from what we've delivered in Years 1 and 2, it could potentially be costly or force us to renegotiate. We're close to having a really good agreement, but I think we still have a few issues to address.
>
> Luc

Luc flags his areas of concern clearly, but his e-mail sounds more like he's turning over some thoughts in his head than actually making a suggestion. What does Luc want from his readers? Does he know at this point?

Now suppose Luc looks at this first draft, thinks about what he's really asking, and does some revising.

> I think we're close to a really good agreement with SARCO. But I suggest we hold off finalizing the contract until we clarify these two questions:
>
> * What exactly is the sign-off process? (We tried but didn't resolve it on the call.)
> * What are the requirements for Year 3?

If we don't straighten these out now, it could be costly in the
future. Let's put these on the agenda for the next call and push to
get resolution.
Luc

The content of the two e-mails is nearly the same, but in the second
draft Luc has taken a moment to clarify in his own mind exactly why
he's sending the message: he wants to hold off on signing the contract
and continue discussions with SARCO until the two open issues are
clarified. The team knows where he stands, he's made a concrete suggestion, and now everyone can get to a resolution faster.

Of course there are situations where you might not want to be as
direct as Luc has been in his second draft, maybe for political reasons.
If you're going to propose something you know will be unpopular, for
instance, you might choose to be less direct and soften your message a
bit. Whether you choose to be direct or indirect in your communication, you should do it by choice, not by accident.

We're often in such a rush that we fire off e-mails without much
thought—we think they're clear, but are they? If your ask isn't clear
in your own mind, your chances of expressing it clearly are slim.
You're likely to wander, let your focus drift, and lose your reader's
attention.

A lot of our communications at work are less high-stakes than Luc's
e-mail. Many are simply about conveying information. But even if the
stakes aren't particularly high, you'd like your reader to actually *read*
your message, and getting your ask clear can help make that happen.

Let's look at a second example of getting the ask clear. In this case,
Harshita is writing to her boss, Lyn, to share information about a
workshop she thinks might be useful for their team.

Hi Lyn,
I had lunch yesterday with Len Cohen. I don't know if you've
heard of him, but he was the company's director of visual

communications for over twenty years, and he's still giving workshops in visual design, using charts, and creating effective presentations. I'm attaching some of the materials he sent me. I'd love to chat with you about his workshops one of these days.

Thanks,

Harshita

Do you think Lyn is going to open those attachments? I don't. She might mean to, but she probably never will. Harshita fired off this e-mail in a hurry, without thinking of the outcome she wanted. If Harshita really wants Lyn to look at the information, she'll craft a message with that purpose in mind:

Hi Lyn,

I had lunch yesterday with Len Cohen. I don't know if you've heard of him, but he was the company's director of visual communications for over twenty years, and he's still giving workshops in visual design, using charts, and creating effective presentations. I'm attaching some of the materials he sent me. I think the Communicating Through Presentations workshop could be really helpful for us. Let's talk.

Thanks,

Harshita

This version is likely to pique Lyn's interest, and she'll be more liable to look at the information. Now let's take it a step further and imagine that Harshita thinks it would be a really great idea for the team to take one of these workshops. So her ask has changed from simply sharing information to trying to convince Lyn to consider booking the workshop. (Note that I said convince her to *consider*. It's too early to convince her to *say yes*. The more precisely you understand the ask for each communication, the better your chance of communicating effectively.)

Hi Lyn,

What would you think about getting the team some training in presenting? I'm attaching information about a workshop I think the team could benefit from, and I'd love to talk with you about it.

I had lunch yesterday with Len Cohen. I don't know if you've heard of him, but he was the company's director of visual communications for over twenty years, and he's still giving workshops in visual design, using charts, and creating effective presentations.

I think his Communicating Through Presentations workshop would be great for us. A lot of our team hasn't come up through the sales organization, so they didn't get the kind of grounding that others have (this includes me). I think it would be especially helpful for our sales team. But as we grow, we want everyone to be comfortable presenting. Shall I block half an hour next week to talk about this?

Thanks,

Harshita

In this version, Harshita is clear in her mind what she wants to do: get Lyn interested in this material and begin a discussion about whether to hire Len. How does she do that? She opens the e-mail with a question for Lyn—Lyn now knows she's supposed to make a decision about this topic rather than just read about it. Harshita uses a more engaged and enthusiastic tone. She also makes a clear recommendation ("I think his . . . workshop would be great for us"), coupled with support for that recommendation (pointing out that the team lacks this skill and that everyone needs to be able to present because the group is growing so fast).

So you can see how taking a minute to clarify what you want and construct your message accordingly can result in very different messages—with potentially very different results.

How to Get the Ask Clear

Most of us are short on time when we write at work, and we don't have much opportunity to craft our messages. But it usually takes less than a minute to stop and think about what you're asking from your readers and to write your message with that objective in mind. When you consider how much time you might waste waiting for a reply that doesn't come or sorting out any confusion that might follow an unclear ask, it's well worth spending that minute to clarify your purpose before you hit Send.

If you're a **planner** and like to organize your content before you write a draft, try this trick as you're planning. Say to yourself:

> *I am writing because* _____.
> *I want my reader to* _____.

Fill in those blanks as specifically as you can. Don't do it thoughtlessly—imagine exactly what you want your reader to do in response to your message. It might sound like a silly exercise, but you'll be amazed at how this little bit of clarity will stop you from writing long, vague, ineffective messages.

If you're the type who likes to **edit**, and you already have a draft complete, stop before you send it off. Ask yourself:

> *What is my purpose in writing this?*
> *What do I want from my reader?*

If you can't answer these questions, or if your answers seem vague, take a minute and think it through. Then try to put yourself in your reader's shoes, and ask:

> *Will my purpose be clear to my reader?*

If the answer is no, take some time to rework what you've written. This process often involves rewriting the beginning of the document to orient your reader (we'll look more at beginnings in Step 3, *Start strong and specific*), cutting down the content, and doing some reorganizing to present your ideas in a structured way.

SUMMARY: Get the Ask Clear

* Think for a moment before you start to write or before you finalize. Ask yourself, "What outcome do I want from this? What do I want my reader to do?"
* Then ask yourself, "Have I really made it clear what I want my reader to do?"
* Put yourself in your reader's shoes as you scan your draft for clarity. Will she understand the ask?
* Write or revise your draft so that it's clear to the reader what you want, why you want it, and what he should do next.

In the next step, we'll look more closely at your reader, with a focus on understanding her needs and tailoring your message to appeal to her.

Ask a Colleague for Help

If you're working on a document or message that's important to you, consider asking for help. Find a colleague you trust, and ask him to read over your draft and share his impressions of how it's working. Having a second set of eyes on your draft can help you see what you might be missing. Whenever you ask a colleague to read a draft, make sure you direct his attention to areas where you want help: Is it persuasive? Is it too long? Do I need to say more? Is the tone okay? If you just plop the text in front of him, you'll probably get feedback on things that don't matter to you. People want to be helpful (and they want to sound smart), so you'll get a more comprehensive review than you need, and your colleague might even miss what you're looking for. You'll save your colleague's time as well as your own by asking specific questions about the draft. Don't forget to offer to return the favor. It's great to have a trusted partner at work when you need editing or even just a quick proofread.

Propose a Solution

Do you want to be a better writer and a better colleague? If you're writing about a problem and you're not sure of the solution, don't just speculate and don't just shift it back to someone else—propose a solution.

How aggressively you pursue this strategy will depend on a few different variables: the culture in your organization, your position, and the position of your reader, among other things. Proposing a solution might mean making a strong argument for a particular course of action, or it might mean sharing your opinion. Whatever course you choose, you'll be giving your readers something to respond to rather than just pointing out a problem and leaving it for someone else to deal with. By proposing a solution, you help everyone get closer to solving the problem faster.

How to Write by Avoiding Writing

Joel Comm

A lot of people are afraid to write, but not me. I'll tell you why. I've figured out how to write by not writing.

I have a lot of projects I'm working on at the same time, including writing a new book, and to be honest I find the process of writing books agonizing. It's a huge task. But I love telling stories, and I love talking about ideas. So I've found a way to harness what I'm good at to get my writing done. I sit down with someone who asks really good questions, and in answering those questions, I tell the stories and talk about the ideas I want to include in my book. Once this process is done, I have the content transcribed and work with an associate to make sense of it.

This same technique can work for you, especially if you're intimidated by the act of writing. If you have something to write that's making you nervous or something you really don't want to write, grab someone you trust in your office, and talk it through. Ask them to ask you questions. Get the juices flowing. Stir up the conversation, and let it draw the content out of you. Take notes if you want to, but don't get so bogged down in the note-taking that you fail to engage in the dialogue. If you're going to take notes, it's better to jot down any especially good key phrases that pop out of your mouth rather than try to write down every word. The idea is to keep your thought process flowing.

Speaking rather than writing is a technique that executives used regularly years ago, dictating letters and other documents into a Dictaphone or speaking while their secretaries took notes in shorthand. They trusted their secretaries to transcribe accurately and to clean up any grammatical errors that might have slipped out.

While most of us don't have assistants who take dictation, this technique is still something you can make a habit of. Find a thinking/writing/telling partner at work, someone you trust, and help each other; listen and ask good questions to support each other with writing tasks. You'll find that you can get your writing done more easily by avoiding writing.

Joel Comm is a New York Times *best-selling author, professional key-note speaker, social media marketing strategist, live video expert, technologist, brand influencer, and futurist.*

STEP 2: WRITE FOR YOUR READER

"There are different kinds of writing for different audiences and different purposes—too often people forget the real audience and just write generically, as if there were no reader there."

—SURVEY RESPONDENT

Understanding and articulating what you want is only half of the communication formula. The other half, of course, is your reader. If your ask is clear, your reader should understand what you want him to do. Now it's time to work on convincing him to do it. To do that, you have to **write for your reader**.

It's surprising how easy it is to forget about your reader. If you're just firing off a short e-mail, your reader is probably at the top of your mind—e-mail is a lot like conversation that way. But the longer and more complex your document gets, the more likely you are to lose sight of your reader. You're managing a lot of content, you're probably in a rush, and it's easy to get sucked into saying what you want to say instead of what the reader needs to hear, or trying to present comprehensive information, or presenting information just because you have it. Especially if you've been involved in researching or otherwise obtaining the information, the impulse is often to include more than your reader really needs.

Whether you're planning a document or editing a draft, it's crucial for you to look at it from your reader's point of view. Each reader has a unique point of view, and the better you understand that point of view, the more successful your communication will be. There are three factors you need to consider if you want to understand your reader's point of view:

* **Relationship.** What's your relationship with your reader? Is your reader your boss, your client, your subordinate? Does your reader have to do as you ask, or do you have to convince him?
* **Information.** How much information does your reader have about the topic you're writing about? How much do you need to supply? How much information does your reader need to take the action you'd like her to take?
* **Attitude.** What is your reader likely to think about your message? Will he be enthusiastic, cautious, hostile, indifferent? What expectations will he have? What's in it for him?

These three factors are often intertwined, but thinking about them separately can help you understand the impact of each one. Let's look at some examples of how each of these factors might affect the way you write.

Relationship

Your relationship with your reader will shape the content you provide in your message and the way you provide it. Let's look at an example.

Mathias works for an IT consulting firm and is becoming worried that his client is withholding information from him. He's writing to his boss, Cherie, and to his client contact, Rich, to try to solve the problem.

Hi Cherie,
I'm running up against a problem with the sales group, particularly Rich. I think he's withholding information about some transactions. I suspect the margin on some of their complex deals was not as good as it should have been. Oversight has been poor, so they've been able to keep this under wraps. We can't complete the analysis unless we have complete information, and any recommendations we make will be skewed if we have bad data. I'll follow up with Rich and keep you posted.
Mathias

And here Mathias raises the same issue with his client contact, Rich:

Hi Rich,
I was reviewing the data last night, and I'm having trouble tracking down a couple of deals. We want to look at all the transactions in aggregate, so I'm not worried about focusing on the details of any single transaction, but we do need to have data on all of them. Can you help me find the info on the Morton and Julu deals? Happy to jump on the phone if that would help.
    Thanks,
    Mathias

Mathias has to walk a fine line here and address the needs of these two different readers. With his boss, Cherie, he can be blunt about what he suspects: that someone at the client is hiding data to protect himself. He also has to let her know what's at risk from her point of view: that incomplete data can affect the results of their analysis and cause them to deliver inferior recommendations. With the client contact, Rich, Mathias has to raise the issue of the missing data in a non-threatening way in order to get cooperation—he can't force Rich to hand over the information. Mathias tells Rich that they are looking at the data in aggregate rather than studying the details of individual deals, which should reassure Rich that they will not be focusing on any mistakes he might have made.

There's no guarantee that Rich will cooperate, and there's no way to reassure Rich that he won't be held to account for any problems with his deals, but Mathias has done his best to anticipate Rich's concerns and allay them.

Information

Different readers need different kinds of information. Let's look at a couple of examples.

José works for Avalantra, a pharmaceutical company that's developed a new extended-release formulation of the popular medication skeezazine, Skeezixx XR. His boss has asked him to draft scripts for two animated videos to be used on the company's website: one for patients, which will be placed on the home page, and another for doctors, which will appear on a special password-protected page for providers on the site.

José knows that these two audiences both need to be introduced to the new medication but that they're going to require slightly different information because they have different needs and points of view. He tackles the version for doctors first:

> New Skeezixx XR offers your skeezazine patients more options, with a $0 co-pay and a streamlined prescribing process. Skeezixx XR is the only 100% extended-release bead formulation of skeezazine. Skeezixx XR's unique formulation delivers smooth skeezazine levels over a 24-hour period with the convenience of once-daily dosing. And Skeezixx XR is available in a broader range of dosage options than any other brand, with five available formulations—25 mg, 50 mg, 100 mg, 150 mg, and 200 mg.
>
> The Skeezixx XR **Quick Start Program** is designed to ensure that your patients have access to affordable Avalantra medications. The program can quickly identify patients eligible for a $0 co-pay offer. This offer is available automatically at pharmacies nationwide through an e-voucher. Our agents can help patients locate pharmacies where the e-voucher is available.
>
> It's never been so simple to prescribe Skeezixx XR.

Now the version for patients:

> Getting the Skeezixx XR you need has never been easier. The Skeezixx XR Quick Start Program is designed to ensure that you have access to affordable Avalantra medications. You may be eligible for a $0 co-pay offer, and if your insurance requires prior authorization, we can provide free products to help you get started immediately.

In addition, we offer personal assistance that works with your insurance from start to finish to gain prior authorization. Our Pharmacy Services team can also fill your first prescription and send it directly to your home.

Finally, we offer patient assistance to qualified patients. Patients whose insurance denies coverage or who are paying cash may be able to get Skeezixx XR for an affordable discounted price.

It's never been so simple to get the skeezazine formulation you need. Talk to your doctor about Skeezixx XR!

You can see that these different versions reflect the needs and interests of their respective audiences. Patients don't need the detailed information about available dosages or all the ins and outs of the prescribing options that are essential for doctors. Patients do need to know that Avalantra is going to make the medication accessible to them.

Now let's look at a more day-to-day example of providing the right information for different audiences.

Darlene's small company is finally getting around to digitizing all its customer records, and she's decided to have her current staff do data entry from the paper files, supported by a couple of temps. Here Darlene writes to the staff members who will be working on the project:

Hi all,

Thanks so much for stepping up to get the legacy files digitized. It will be great to have everything in one place.

We'll be starting on Monday, with the objective of finishing by Friday the 23rd. Xiomara will assign you the files to work on.

You should use the regular customer system with your regular login. Please follow these procedures:

1. Before you enter anything, check to ensure that there is not an existing record for the customer. If you find significant discrepancies between the paper files and the existing records, please ask Xiomara or me.

2. Please enter the following fields from the paper files:

Name

Address

Phone

Contact person

Dates served. If you are not sure about the close date, leave that field blank.

Rep(s) who served the customer

If you have any questions at all, please ask Xiomara or me. I mean this. Don't guess when you have questions. The whole point of this is to clean up our records. It's worth taking a little extra time to figure out how to do it right.

Thank you again! I really appreciate your willingness to work on this project.

Best,

Darlene

Darlene also needs to orient the temps who will be helping the staff with the data entry project:

Hi,

Welcome to the team, and thank you for signing on to work on this project. As I'm sure you know, we're working to digitize all our customer records. You'll be working alongside our regular employees to get these records entered into our database.

We'll be starting on Monday, with the objective of finishing by Friday the 23rd.

Before we get into the details of the data entry, some information about the system.

You should have received your login credentials in the introductory e-mail. If you did not, please let me know immediately. If you forget your login, please notify me.

The system will log you out after ten minutes of inactivity.

However, I would ask that you not walk away from the screen without logging out. If you need to step away for any reason, please log out and log back in when you return.

The system autosaves, but please make it a habit to hit Save (in the upper right of the screen) after each entry.

Xiomara Maldonado will assign you the files to work on.

Please follow these procedures:

1. Before you enter anything, check to ensure that there is not an existing record for the customer. If you find significant discrepancies between the paper files and existing records—variations on company names, different addresses, etc.—please ask Xiomara or me.
2. Please enter the following fields from the paper files:
    Name
    Address
    Phone
    Contact person
    Dates served. If you are not sure about the close date, leave that field blank.
    Rep(s) who served the customer

If you have any questions at all, please ask Xiomara or me. **Please do not guess** when you have questions. **We would rather have you ask than guess.**

Thank you again! I really appreciate your willingness to work on this project.

Best,

Darlene

Darlene has used the message to her staff as the basis for this message to the temps, and she's thought carefully about what additional information the temps might need. She's added some context for the project and some information about how the database system works. She's also rewritten point 1 so that it's clearer to a reader who's not part of the team. And she's rewritten the section about asking rather than guessing for the audience of temps. In taking the time to customize the message for the temps, she's prevented a lot of confusion and probably a lot of errors.

We'll take another look at choosing the right content for your message in Step 5, *Fill in missing content; delete extraneous content* (page 68).

How Writing a Business Plan Can Make You a Better Business Writer
Robert C. Daugherty

Today's hottest companies—from Amazon to Apple to Google—have at least one thing in common: they all started with a business plan. A business plan is a document written for potential investors that outlines objectives and strategies; it is intended to convince investors to put up cash for the new enterprise. The stakes are very high: you *must* address your reader's concerns, or you won't get the funding you need to start your business.

To write a successful business plan, you have to provide persuasive answers to three sets of questions. First are the people questions: Why are you the person to launch and run this business? Are you known in the market? Can you attract the talent needed for success? Second are the opportunity questions: Is the market for your product or service large and growing? Is there a good fit between the product and the market? And third are the environment questions: What is the context in which the venture is being launched? Are there competitors entering the market? How will you respond when the market changes (and it will)? Your answers to these questions can mean the difference between a successful, funded business and a lost opportunity. If you fail to answer them adequately, your reader will simply say thanks, but no thanks.

Imagine if you took the same kind of approach to your every-day business writing tasks, understanding that if you didn't meet your readers' expectations, you simply wouldn't get what you were asking for. Imagine if you asked yourself questions like "What does my reader care about?" and "How can I supply what my reader needs?" and "How can I convince my reader?" every time you wrote an important message. Obviously, most situations at work don't have such high stakes, but the practice of writing a business plan imposes a discipline that's useful for all kinds of business writing. Focus on your everyday business writing with the same kind of attention and intensity entrepreneurs use in crafting a business plan, and you'll increase your success rate with all your business communications.

Robert C. Daugherty is the executive dean of the Forbes School of Business and Technology.

Attitude

Sarah works for a small retailer whose website has expanded dramatically over the past few years. The website began as a supplement to the company's print catalog years ago, and now it's the primary sales channel. Sarah wants her boss, Mary, to provide some help for the team maintaining the website content.

Hi Mary,

We really need help with the website. We can't keep up with the volume of changes to the product descriptions on the site. Initially it made sense to have the marketing assistant maintain these. But since we've expanded so much, I think it's time to take another look.

Jamie is swamped. In addition, we have so many different

product categories now that we don't have a consistent template for them or a consistent voice. There's information missing from product descriptions, and Jamie is having to deal with the phone inquiries that come in.

I think we should consider bringing in a contractor for the specific purpose of cleaning up all the product descriptions and posting new ones as we go forward. We could probably use a person full-time to take care of the site and the product descriptions, but as a first step we could bring in a contractor. Jamie and I could create a template and try to round up the missing content as the contractor identifies it.

Do you have time to talk about this next week?

Thanks,

Sarah

Sarah is understandably frustrated by the situation. It sounds like Jamie's job has grown, and he needs some help. If you look at Sarah's attitude in this draft, she's focused almost exclusively on what she needs, and she hasn't taken into account what Mary's attitude might be.

What might Mary think about Sarah's message? First, it's going to cost her money to hire a contractor. Even more alarmingly to anyone who has to manage a budget, Sarah's talking about hiring another full-time permanent employee. Sarah's message leaves some important questions unanswered. Sarah says Jamie is swamped, but why? And if Sarah and Jamie have the time to create a template and find the new content, why can't they handle updating the descriptions? If I were Mary, my first response would be "No."

Sarah hasn't thought about this likely response, because she hasn't fully considered what Mary's attitude toward the idea might be. She's thought only of what she and her team need. Now let's say she's taken some time to consider her reader in addition to her ask, and she's going to write for her reader.

Hi Mary,

Can we set aside some time next week to talk about managing the website? We've expanded so much that the job has outgrown the way we initially conceived it, and I think bringing in a part-time contractor might meet our needs without being too expensive.

We're having the following problems:

* Product descriptions on the site aren't consistent, especially across categories.
* These inconsistent product descriptions result in an inconsistent voice online, so we're not really implementing the branding work we did last year.
* There's content missing in a lot of product descriptions, and Jamie is spending a lot of time fielding phone inquiries.
* Inconsistent and incomplete product descriptions make for a poor online experience for customers.
* Jamie is spending his time playing catch-up rather than advancing our marketing. He's smart and has good ideas, and we didn't hire him to do data entry or answer phones.

Here's what I suggest:

* You, Jamie, and I should work on a template for product descriptions that reflects the brand personality we came up with last year.
* Once we have that, we could hire a part-time person on a contract basis to go through the site, pull the product descriptions into compliance with the new template, and flag any missing content.
* Once we've cleaned things up, we can decide where to go from there.

I'll follow up tomorrow to see if we can put something on the calendar.

Thanks!

Sarah

In this revised version, Sarah has thought about Mary's potential response. What's in it for Mary now? More than just more money going out the door. The current proposal creates an opportunity to implement the branding they've already invested in, a better experience online for customers, and the potential to use Jamie for what he was hired to do. Sarah has thought more about the situation and realized that they might not need the contractor forever, and they might not need another full-time person—but if they do, Mary will understand why.

Writing for a Group of Readers

Writing for your reader is straightforward when you have just one reader. It becomes more complicated when you're writing for a group. In a situation like that, you have to assume that your readers might have different points of view and, perhaps, different needs. How do you strategize when you're writing for a group of readers? To help focus your efforts, try asking yourself some questions: Which of your readers is the most senior? Who's the decision-maker? Who's going to be the hardest to convince? Who's likely to object and why? Once you've done this analysis, you can anticipate readers' objections.

But what if you're writing for a group that includes people you don't know, as often happens when you're submitting a proposal? In that sort of situation, take a page from the marketers' book and create personas—fictional readers who are typical of the kinds of people reading your writing. For instance, you might imagine a more senior manager than the one you're submitting the proposal to. You might imagine a reader concerned about budget. You might picture a reader who has another solution in mind. Don't let yourself become overwhelmed by thinking about all of these potential readers; rather, use your insights about them to make sure your writing addresses each of their needs, at least in a preliminary way. Don't let them freak you out; let them help you. When you're writing for a group, thinking about your potential readers can help you anticipate reasonable objections and make a stronger argument in the process.

How to Write for Your Reader

If you like to **plan** before you write, the following trick can help you craft your message to appeal to your reader. In Step 1, *Get the ask clear,* you did an exercise designed to help pinpoint your purpose in writing. Now take what you did there and expand it. As you plan your draft, try completing these two very useful sentences:

My purpose is to _____ so that my reader will _____.
My reader needs to understand _____ to be able to do that.

If you're an **editor** rather than a planner and have a draft you're revising, try reading your draft from your reader's point of view. Ask yourself:

If I were [insert name of reader], I would think _____.
If I were [insert name of reader], I would want to know _____.
If I were [insert name of reader], I would react better if _____.

For both planners and editors, putting yourself in your reader's shoes can help you anticipate objections and connect more successfully with your reader.

Writing for Global Teams

With the rise of virtual teaming, many of us are now frequently working with people from other countries and other cultures. And because those team members live in diverse places, our only interaction with them might be in writing. When you're working with a global team, take some precautions to help promote understanding and prevent offense.

Here are a few tips that can keep global teams communicating smoothly:

* Get everyone's name right. You might find yourself on a team with people who have names that are unfamiliar to you. Take the time to learn how to spell and pronounce everyone's name correctly. If you're not sure, ask; people would rather be asked than have their names mangled.
* Avoid using jargon. Even for people who know English very well, some business jargon—especially jargon based in metaphor—might not make much sense. Instead of writing, "let's not boil the ocean," write, "let's not do more work than we need to do." Instead of suggesting that the team start with "low-hanging fruit," suggest they start with "problems that are easy to solve." (Even when you're writing for a domestic audience, it's a good idea to keep expressions like this to a minimum.)
* If someone writes something you don't understand, take the time to clarify it. Don't assume you know what it means—ask.
* Tread carefully around saying no. Some cultures are uncomfortable with refusing requests and otherwise saying no. In some cultures, a direct refusal can cause people

to lose face, so bad news is delivered indirectly. If your colleague seems to be communicating vaguely or not answering questions, they might be trying to say no without coming right out and saying it. Try rephrasing your question, summarizing what you think your colleague means, and being gently persistent to be sure you understand what the message really is.

* Give everyone the benefit of the doubt. If someone's tone sounds peculiar to you, you might just be reacting to a different cultural norm.

* Always err on the side of courtesy. It's better to be a bit more formal than usual than to risk hurting someone's feelings.

Anticipate Objections

There's a strategic element to most communication, even if the stakes don't seem very high. Part of strategy is anticipating and preempting the moves of the other. If you're writing to try to get something from someone—whether it's a sale, funding for a project, or an agreement to an approach—it's smart to think about how your reader is likely to respond and anticipate any objections they might raise.

Anticipating objections requires really understanding your reader, so that you can see the matter from her point of view. Is she in charge of the budget? What other demands is she facing? Why should she allocate money to your project rather than to others? What other demands is he dealing with besides your request? Will he have time to address your issue on top of everything else? How can you make your issue a priority for him, given his competing priorities? Is this a bad time for the organization to take risks? How can you convince your reader that the upside outweighs the potential downside? Anticipating and addressing objections in advance can help prevent the reader from rejecting your idea out of hand, and it can shorten any discussion or negotiation that might follow your initial communication.

The "You" Attitude

The "you" attitude is an approach to business communication developed by the late Kitty O. Locker, a professor of English at Ohio State University.* Put simply, the "you" attitude in writing puts the focus on the reader rather than on the writer. It highlights the importance of the reader and calls out benefits to them. Implementing the "you" attitude in your writing often involves changing the subject of the sentence from "I" or "we" to "you":

We are shipping your order	→	*You will receive your order*
We have the largest selection	→	*You can choose from the largest selection*

As you can see, sales writers have understood this approach for a long time, but you don't have to be selling anything to make a bid for your reader's attention in this way. The "you" attitude is useful in any situation where you want to harness your reader's goodwill:

We need your help to	→	*You can help by*
Our new process takes only 15 minutes	→	*You can get through the new process in only 15 minutes*
I can finish this faster if you	→	*You'll get a faster result if*

A shift in focus from "I" to "you" is an easy trick to make your writing more appealing and engage your reader.

*Professor Locker coauthored (with Donna Kienzler) the textbook *Business and Administrative Communication* (11th edition; New York: McGraw-Hill Education, 2015).

Use Formatting to Guide Your Reader

Part of writing for your reader is doing your best to ensure that your message is easy to understand. In addition to selecting content carefully, you can make your message more accessible by using formatting that will help your reader absorb your message. Most people at work don't really read text—they scan it. These three tricks can make text more easily scannable and highlight content that might be important to your reader:

* Use short paragraphs. The eye tends to "bounce" off text set in long paragraphs. A series of paragraphs of **a few sentences each** will be much easier for your reader to scan.
* Use bulleted lists. Whenever you have **a list of items**, consider formatting it as a bulleted list. The list might be single words, sentences, or questions. A word of caution: don't try to force content into bulleted lists if the elements aren't parallel or if they need fuller development than a simple list can provide. Some business writers have gone overboard with the bullets—if you use them, make sure they make sense.
* Use strategic bolding. Strategic bolding **highlights important words** and **draws the reader's eye to them**. If a passage has effective strategic bolding, the reader should be able to **glance at it and get the gist of it**, rather than reading it word for word. As with bullet points, be careful not to overdo it. **If you bold too much** of your text, the bolding becomes meaningless noise and **can have the opposite of the intended effect**.

A final word of caution: don't go nuts with any of these formatting techniques. If your text is too full of bulleted lists, bolding, and italics, it's going to look like a sales letter. You also risk organizing your writing around the formatting, rather than focusing on developing the content itself. Use formatting as a tool and let it serve you, rather than your serving it. When used skillfully, formatting can help you organize content and direct your reader's eye to what's really important.

SUMMARY: Write for Your Reader

As you think about how you can meet your reader's needs and expectations, consider these variables:

* **Relationship:** Who is my reader, and what is her relationship to me? Does she have to do what I ask?
* **Information:** How much information does my reader have about my topic? How much background do I have to supply to help him understand? What kind of information will appeal to him?
* **Attitude:** What is my reader's likely attitude to what I'm saying? Will she be receptive or resistant? What information do I need to include to persuade her?

In the next step, we'll look at the beginning of your document and explore how a strong and specific opening can pique your readers' interest and motivate them to keep reading.

STEP 3: START STRONG AND SPECIFIC

"I wish some of my co-workers would get to the point faster. There is too much introduction and justification before they get to the point."

—SURVEY RESPONDENT

A lot of people have trouble writing introductions and other openings. Getting started on anything can be challenging. It can be especially difficult when you're trying to introduce a message or document that doesn't exist yet—that is, writing an introduction before you've written the rest of the draft.

But beginnings make a big impression. Readers typically decide within seconds how they're going to deal with a message or document. If your document starts out loose and sloppy and meandering, you risk losing your reader's attention. To engage your reader and motivate her to continue reading, you need to **start strong and specific**.

A good opening should:

* Capture your reader's attention
* Let your reader know what's coming and why it's important
* Let your reader know what he's supposed to do: absorb information, respond, or take some kind of action
* Motivate your reader to continue reading through the end

Let's look at a few examples of not-so-compelling beginnings and see how they might be improved.

Team,
I reviewed the development timeline, and there are several outstanding issues to resolve before we go live. Due to travel

schedules, feedback on the prototype came in later than expected. The new polymer components requested will not be available till April 10. This pushes the timeline out to a period when the vendor cannot turn around our request in a timely way—their next window to work on the project is April 16–19.

I think we can catch up by combining the beta verification period with the beta review. This means we will do verification and review April 19–20. Please let me know what you think.

Thanks,

Abhi

Abhi does a good job of outlining the "issues to resolve," but his opening doesn't indicate the consequences of the problem and isn't specific. He decides to revise his message so that his readers will know what's at stake right away:

Team,

I reviewed the development timeline, and at our current pace we are going to miss the go-live date. To catch up, I propose combining the beta verification period with the beta review: both can occur April 19–20. Please let me know if this is OK.

Outstanding issues include:

* Late feedback on the prototype (due to travel schedules)
* New polymer components not available till April 10
* Vendor does not have availability till April 16–19

Please let me know if we can do the combined verification/ review April 19–20.

Thanks,

Abhi

This version is much better. Abhi captures his readers' attention right away by letting them know what's at stake: they're at risk of missing the final deadline on the project. He proposes his solution in the second sentence, and he asks the readers to respond in the third sentence. He's front-loaded all the important information into a concise first paragraph with a clear ask of the reader. He's also put the outstanding issues into a bulleted list so they're easy to scan, making it easier for the reader to grasp the situation and respond to it.

Let's look at another example.

> Jessica,
>
> We need to make some arrangements for Dalia's maternity leave. Right now she is saying she wants to take six weeks, but I think we should have a plan in place in case she decides she needs to be out longer—policy allows her up to twelve.
>
> We'll need coverage for the front desk, processing the incoming mail, and supporting Carl at the open house events.
>
> We can break things out this way:
>
> ✳ Front desk: I think we should get a temp for the high-traffic times, which are Monday–Thursday. The rest of the staff could cover as needed on Fridays.
> ✳ Processing mail: Let's pick one staff member to own this and have Dalia train them.
> ✳ Open houses: Staff could rotate. Bob, Liang, Steph, and Esme have all worked on these in the past and could potentially fill in. Am I forgetting anyone?
>
> I'd love your input on these ideas. Dalia is planning to go out on May 7, so we should have a plan in place within the next two weeks.
> Thanks,
> Eric

Eric does a good job of laying out the impact of Dalia's maternity leave and proposing some solutions, but if Jessica just skims the beginning of this message, she won't understand the urgency of the situation or that Eric is asking for her response. Eric doesn't let Jessica know till the last sentence that they have only two weeks to make arrangements to cover Dalia's duties. Dalia's looming departure is a big deal for him, but it might not be for Jessica. It's better for him to be explicit about the need and the urgency rather than making assumptions about what Jessica knows and thinks.

Now let's look at Eric's revised version:

Jessica,

Below are some ideas for coverage for Dalia's maternity leave—please let me know your reaction to them. She is going out May 7, so we need to have a plan ready to go in two weeks. Right now she is saying she wants to take six weeks, but I think we should have a plan in place in case she decides she needs to be out longer—policy allows her up to twelve, so she might be out until July 30.

We'll need coverage for the front desk, processing the incoming mail, and supporting Carl at the open house events.

We could break things out this way:

* Front desk: I think we should get a temp for the high-traffic times, which are Monday–Thursday. The rest of the staff could cover as needed on Fridays.
* Processing mail: Let's pick one staff member to own this and have Dalia train them.
* Open houses: Staff could rotate. Bob, Liang, Steph, and Esme have all worked on these in the past and could potentially fill in. Am I forgetting anyone?

I'll follow up with you next week.
Thanks,
Eric

In this version, Eric has made the opening of his message strong and specific: there is time pressure, and he's offering suggestions that he wants Jessica's opinion about. He begins his message by letting Jessica know that there is information below she needs to read and respond to, thus motivating her to read the whole message.

How to Start Strong and Specific

Beginnings can be difficult, but there are a couple of ways you can take the pressure off when it comes to writing your openings. First, be aware that you don't have to write your beginning first (see the box "You Don't Have to Start at the Beginning" on page 46). Second, it's always a good idea to go back and revise your opening after you've completed a full draft. If you make a habit of revising your beginning before you finalize your document, you can be sure not only that your opening is attractive to readers but also that it accurately represents what follows in the rest of the document.

If you're the type of writer who likes to **plan** before you write, take a minute and ask yourself:

How can I grab my reader?
What will make my reader want to keep reading?

In Step 2, you spent some time analyzing your reader. Use what you learned in that step to plan an opening that will appeal to him. What will your reader think is important about this message? A **risk/opportunity analysis** is a good place to start: Is there **risk** your reader wants to avoid? Is there an **opportunity** he doesn't want to miss? Whatever that issue is, figure out how to get it up front in your message or document. You don't have to explain all the details of the issue at the beginning, but you do have to raise it. Once you have the opening planned, think about how you can arrange your content to motivate readers to continue reading. Sometimes it's as easy as saying something like "I'm proposing three potential solutions below." Whatever you do, don't bury important information—such as deadline and next steps—at the end. Front-load as much as you can, fill in the details in the middle, and use your conclusion as a reinforcement.

If you're an **editor**, the type of writer who likes to draft first and then revise, be sure you go back to the beginning of your draft with a critical eye. Put yourself in your reader's shoes, and ask:

Is this something I'd want to read?
Would I read through to the end of this message?

If the answer is no, consider how you might grab your reader's attention. Is there an opportunity or risk you can bring to the fore to get her attention? Can you say something in the beginning to motivate her to read the whole thing?

No matter if you're writing a quick e-mail or a long report, it's important to be sure your opening is clear and that you're saying it in a way that will catch your reader's attention.

Whether you're a **planner** or an **editor**, it's a good idea to double-check your opening before you send your document off to the reader. Especially with longer documents, ideas often shift while you're writing, and your original opening might not accurately reflect what follows. When you review, you might have more clarity about your purpose and how you're going to appeal to your reader. As you review, ask yourself:

Is it clear to my reader why I'm writing?
Is my reader incentivized to keep reading?
Does my tone support my message? (For more information on
    tone, see the box "Does This Sound Okay?" on page 92.)

SUMMARY: Start Strong and Specific

* The beginning of your message is make or break. Use your opening to let readers know quickly what to expect.
* Think from your reader's point of view when you write your openings. What will make them want to read? Consider any risks or opportunities you can highlight in the beginning to grab your reader's attention.
* Use your opening to motivate your readers to read beyond the first few lines.
* Go back and check your opening once you've finished your draft. Does it align with what follows?

You Don't Have to Start at the Beginning

Introductions and other kinds of beginnings can be difficult to write. A lot is riding on the opening of your document, and getting started can be intimidating. The good news is that you don't have to start your draft by writing the beginning of it. In fact, the beginning might *not* be the best thing to start with.

Don't get hung up on writing your introduction, especially when you're working on a long document like a report or proposal. Start wherever you feel most confident. That might be somewhere in the middle of the document, a section where you feel you have the most to say or can make the most compelling argument. Go ahead and complete that section, and move on from there. If it helps, you can try writing the document piece by piece, not necessarily in order. Once you have a full draft, you can put the pieces together, smooth out the transitions, and then write the introduction. By this point you'll know exactly what you're introducing, and you'll know what you want to emphasize in your introduction to guide the reader's attention. Very often, introductions that are written last are stronger and more specific than ones that are drafted at the beginning.

In the next step, we'll look at ways to make the best possible use of your reader's time and attention by writing concisely.

STEP 4: BE CONCISE

"Most of the e-mails I get should be 30–50% shorter than they are."

—SURVEY RESPONDENT

In Step 1 you got the ask clear, in Step 2 you tailored your message for your reader, and in Step 3 you wrote a strong beginning. In this step, you'll learn to make your writing more concise.

In the business writing survey I conducted for this book, 87 percent of respondents indicated that writing more concisely was a priority for them, and 63 percent said they wished their colleagues would write more concisely.

The ability to write concisely has a lot of benefits—for your reader, obviously, and also for you. Concise writing tends to get a better response, because your readers will quickly learn what you want. If you get in the habit of writing concisely, you'll spend less time writing and you'll agonize less over what you write. You'll also spend less time following up with people who didn't understand—or didn't even read—what you wrote. Finally, if you make it a habit, you'll get a reputation as someone who's straightforward and doesn't waste people's time—and everyone likes that kind of colleague.

For most of us, writing concisely doesn't come naturally, especially when we're in a hurry. When we're in a rush, we tend to write whatever comes into our heads, and it's often muddy, wordy, and too long. It takes a little time to break the habit of going on too long. As you practice, it begins to come more naturally.

Before we get started, a little caveat: shorter is not *always* better. Sometimes you want a particular tone or style that involves longer sentences, more explanation, or repetition to drive your point home. The key is to do whatever you do—whether writing concisely or more expansively—by choice, not from lack of skill.

Writing concisely involves learning a few editing techniques. There are practically endless ways to edit your writing, and it's easy to feel overwhelmed before you even start. In this section, you'll learn a quick, practical method that will cover about 90 percent of your problems with wordiness. If you want to learn even more, look at the section on editing your own writing later in the book (see page 191).

To give you the power to make your sentences more concise, we're going to look at a little grammar (not too much, I promise). Here are four tips you can use to cut the chaff in your writing:

1. Watch for forms of the verb "to be": ("is," "are," "was," "were," "has been," "have been," etc.).
2. Watch for prepositional phrases.
3. Watch for nominalizations (explained below).
4. Watch for padding.

If you can detect just these four patterns in your own writing and learn to make adjustments when you find them, you will greatly improve your prose and make your readers' lives much easier.

Quick Guide . . .
. . . to Making Your Writing More Concise

❶ Watch for forms of the verb *to be* (am, is, are, was, were, has been, have been)

Turn passive constructions into active ones:

X is done by Y → Y does X

Consider rewriting sentences that begin with *there is, there are, it is.*

❷ Watch for prepositional phrases

If you have strings of phrases beginning with words like *in, on, of, by, around, about,* and *between,* consider rephrasing them:

the permission of the customer → the customer's permission

in many circumstances → often

❸ Watch for nominalizations

"Nominalization" means turning a word into a noun. Typically, nominalizations are verbs that have been turned into nouns, which then require a verb for use in a sentence. Convert these phrases back to the original verbs:

reach an agreement = agree
make a decision = decide
achieve a balance = balance
suffer a loss = lose
have a response = respond
conduct an investigation = investigate
engage in a search = search

❹ Watch for padding

Look out for redundancies:

7 a.m. in the morning
absolutely essential
meet together
basic fundamentals
future plans
final conclusion
lag behind

Look out for "filler" words and phrases that don't add meaning:

actually
in many ways
essentially
at the end of the day
foundationally
ultimately

Don't use a fancy expression where a plain one would do:

utilize → use
initiate → start
in light of the fact that → because
with reference to → about
at this point in time → now

1. Watch for forms of the verb "to be"

The verb "to be" in all its various forms—"I am," "you are," "she or he is," "they are," "we have been"—occurs more frequently than any other verb in English. It's a perfectly fine verb, but relying on it too much can make your sentences longer than they need to be. We'll look at two ways that "to be" can creep into your writing and make it loose and meandering: the **passive voice** and "**there is**" forms.

THE PASSIVE VOICE

Forms of the verb "to be" can signal the presence of the passive voice in your sentence. You've probably heard of the passive voice, but you might not be entirely sure what this sentence structure is. It's called passive because the subject of the sentence is receiving the action of the sentence. Its opposite is the **active voice**, where the subject of the sentence is doing the action of the sentence. The passive voice is formed using the past participle of a verb (often ending in "-ed") and a form of the verb "to be." Because the subject of the sentence isn't doing the action, it's often necessary to add a phrase beginning with "by" to indicate who did it.

Let's look at some examples.

Passive voice: *The intruder* was arrested *by the security guard.*
Active voice: *The security guard* arrested *the intruder.*

In the passive voice version, the subject of the sentence, "the intruder," is being acted upon. In the active version, the subject of the sentence, "security guard," is performing the action.

Passive voice: *Gender and annual income* were cited *by the research as the major drivers of purchase decisions.*
Active voice: *The research* cited *gender and annual income as the major drivers of purchase decisions.*

As you can see, the "action" of a verb isn't always physical action—it's the "doing" part of the sentence. In the example above, "the research" is doing the action, which is *citing*.

Passive: *The beginning of the recession* was signaled *by a sharp dip in stock prices.*
Active*: A sharp dip in stock prices* signaled *the beginning of the recession.*

The action in this example is *signaling*, and it's the dip in stock prices that's doing it.

In all these examples, you can see that the passive version is longer than the active version. Usually it's a difference of just a few words, but if you make a habit of relying on the passive voice and string together a whole paragraph of passive constructions, you can end up with a lot of verbiage you don't need.

Sometimes the actor in a passive sentence is omitted altogether:

*Bus and subway fares **were raised**.* [By whom? Surely not by the MTA?]
*Mistakes **were made** in dealing with the crisis.*
***It was determined** that the proper procedure **had been followed**.*

Looking at examples like these, you can see how using the passive voice might be a handy way to avoid taking responsibility, and some writers use it for exactly that reason.

It's important to point out that passive constructions aren't incorrect. In fact, sometimes they're exactly what you need. You might use a passive construction when you don't know who did the action:

The alarm was tripped at 4:30 this morning.
The fence was blown down for a third time.

And sometimes you genuinely want to emphasize the object of the action, rather than the actor:

Seating arrangements at the event caused some controversy. Corporate representatives sat at the lower tables. The main table was occupied by the mayor and his special guests.

The last sentence in this short passage is in the passive voice, but it's a good choice. It's sensible to make "the main table" the subject of the sentence: the real issue is the seating arrangements, rather than the mayor and his pals.

Although the passive voice is grammatically correct and sometimes preferable, you're usually better off favoring the active voice in business writing. Many business writers fall into the habit of depending on the passive voice because they see other writers doing it. The sound gets into their heads as the proper sound of business and professional writing, and they simply replicate what they hear. However, active constructions have advantages over passive ones: they're shorter, they're more direct, they're easier to read, and they're more engaging. They sound more personal—that impersonal, businessy, "official" tone isn't always what you want—and they create a sense of agency in the sentence: there's a person (or a thing sometimes) who's taking action.

As with any other style choice, your use of the passive or active voice should be your decision rather than something you fall into because you don't know how to control it. Learning to convert passive constructions into active ones, and vice versa, gives you more control over your own writing.

So how do you change a passive construction into an active one? Follow these three steps:

1. Diagnose the passive voice by looking for forms of the verb "to be," like "is," "are," "has been," "have been," and so on, plus the past participle of the verb (usually ending in "-ed"). Passive sentences will sometimes contain phrases beginning with "by" to indicate who or what is doing the action.
2. Ask yourself who or what is *doing* the acting in the sentence, and who or what is *receiving* the action.

3. Flip the sentence so the actor is the subject.

Let's try an example:

The models are used by the teams to project revenue.

1. Form of the verb "to be" followed by a past participle? Yes, "are used."
2. Who or what is doing the acting in the sentence? It's *the teams.*
3. Flip the sentence so that the actor is the subject:

The teams use the models to project revenue.

You can see that the revision isn't just shorter, it's also clearer and more direct.

Here are a few samples for you to practice on. (Solutions are at the bottom of the next page.)

A. *Stress testing is conducted by banks to ensure adequate capital levels.*
B. *The guidelines were rewritten by legal counsel to prevent future breaches.*
C. *Personas are used by marketers to help them understand who their target customers are.*
D. *The faulty monitor was replaced.*

(Notice that in the last sentence, the person doing the replacing doesn't even appear. In your revision, you get to make up who did it.)

"THERE IS," "THERE ARE," "IT IS"

Forms of the verb "to be" can also signal the presence of filler phrases like "there is," "there are," and "it is." These are not passive constructions, and they're not incorrect. However, they don't add meaning, they can create an impersonal and distant feel, and they waste space. Once you learn to spot them, you can tighten up your writing considerably.

> **Original:** *There is a large group of potential customers that can be reached by our affiliate marketing program.*
> **Revised:** *Our affiliate marketing program can reach a large group of potential customers.*

> **Original:** *There are three questions for you to keep in mind.*
> **Revised:** *You should keep three questions in mind.*

> **Original:** *It is under these conditions that the risk is highest.*
> **Revised:** *The risk is highest under these conditions.*

Used occasionally, "there is" and "it is" constructions can help you vary your style and add interest to your writing. As a steady diet, though, they can slow things down and make your writing feel impersonal. Be careful they don't become a habit.

Becoming aware of how you use—or overuse—the verb "to be" can help you tighten and strengthen your writing. Of course, the verb "to be" has plenty of legitimate uses. But when you rely on it too much, your writing can become bloated. Paying attention to your "to be" habits can help you in your quest to make your writing more concise.

2. Watch for prepositional phrases

A preposition is a part of speech defined as "a word or group of words that is used with a noun, pronoun, or noun phrase to show direction, location, or time, or to introduce an object."* That's a pretty vague defi-

---

* *Webster's Ninth New Collegiate Dictionary* (Springfield, Mass., 1983).

A. Banks conduct stress testing to ensure adequate capital levels. B. Legal counsel rewrote the guidelines to prevent future breaches. C. Marketers use personas to help them understand who their target customers are. D. IT replaced the faulty monitor.

nition, and it isn't terrifically helpful on its own. But remembering the definition of prepositions is not as important as your ability to spot them and understand what they do.

Prepositions are those words like "in," "on," "of," "into," "by," "under," "with," "around," "about," and "between" that serve as connectors in a sentence. You'll find a long list of common prepositions in Appendix B. They introduce **prepositional phrases**. A prepositional phrase begins with a preposition and has a noun or a pronoun as the **object of the preposition**. Like so:

about the customer
in the office
on the phone
by my authority
under these circumstances
of the organization

Like the passive voice, prepositional phrases are perfectly correct grammatical forms. It would be hard to write in English without using them. The problem comes when they're overused. When writers try to sound "official," they often fall into the trap of piling up prepositional phrases one after the other. Policy statements and anything else trying to sound legal often feature lots of prepositional phrases strung together. Learning to identify prepositions and the phrases that follow them is an important skill in making your writing more concise, so be on the lookout for phrases beginning with "of," "by," "in," "for," "about," "with," "through," and other prepositions.

Let's look at an example:

Participation in client negotiations with suppliers is prohibited by company policy unless (in very rare circumstances) there is advance consent of a leader of the gyro division in the client's geography as well as an industry leader for the supplier's industry.

Whoa. Most people can recognize this kind of writing as bad. It's a little harder to identify exactly what's wrong (it's prepositional phrases and forms of the verb "to be") and understand how to fix it. Let's take this sentence apart. The prepositional phrases are in italics, and the "to be" forms are in bold:

Participation
in client negotiations
with suppliers
is prohibited
by company policy, unless
(*in very rare circumstances*) **there is** advance consent
of a leader
of the gyro division
in the client's geography as well as an industry leader
for the supplier's industry.

That's a lot of prepositional phrases all strung together. How do we fix it? The first step is to figure out what the message is and say it in plain English.

Here's a colloquial "translation" of the passage:

You can't participate in client negotiations with suppliers unless a leader in the gyro division and a leader in the supplier's industry say it's okay.

That version is probably too informal to use, but doing this kind of commonsense check can help you sort out what's really going on in a sentence burdened with too many prepositional phrases. With only minor revisions, you can turn this version into something you can use:

You may not participate in client negotiations with suppliers unless a leader in the gyro division and a leader in the supplier's industry consent.

Although the prepositional phrases were the main culprit in the sentence, we also cleaned up a couple of forms of the verb "to be." "Participation . . . **is prohibited**" became "you may not participate," and "unless . . . **there is** advance consent" became "unless a leader . . . and a leader . . . consent." (You'll often find loose forms of the verb "to be" in sentences that have strings of prepositional phrases.)

So what's the remedy? Here are three techniques you can use to fix sentences that are overburdened with prepositional phrases:

1. Look for the action in the sentence or clause: What is the action, and who's doing it?

Our original sentence read: "unless there is advance consent of a leader of the gyro division." What's the action there, and who's doing that action? The action is "consent," and the person giving consent is a leader. So we can revise to "unless a leader of the gyro division consents."

2. Replace a prepositional phrase with an adjective:

*the permission **of the client*** → *the **client's** permission*
*members **of the committee*** → ***committee** members*
of a high quality → ***high-quality***

3. Replace a prepositional phrase with an adverb:

in very rare circumstances → *rarely*
in an efficient manner → *efficiently*
with clarity → *clearly*

Once you become attuned to spotting prepositions and prepositional phrases, you'll see them everywhere. Most of them are probably fine. But when you start accumulating a lot of them, you usually end up with unnecessary length. Trimming prepositional phrases can help you make your writing more concise and efficient.

3. Watch for nominalizations

What the heck is "nominalization"? It's taking a verb or adjective, turning it into a noun, and then adding more words to the sentence or phrase to make it mean what it meant in the first place.

Maybe an example would help. Look at the phrases below and see if you can recognize what's going on here:

Reach an agreement = agree
Make a decision = decide
Achieve a balance = balance
Suffer a loss = lose
Have a response = respond
Conduct an investigation = investigate
Have applicability = apply
Engage in a search = search

The words on the right-hand side of the equal signs are all perfectly good verbs that someone felt the need to nominalize—that is, to turn into a noun. Then, because the verb had become a noun, the writer needed an additional verb to do the work needed in the sentence. So because "search" somehow wasn't good enough, someone changed it to "conduct a search," adding words but not meaning.

Nominalization isn't grammatically incorrect, but it's a very common bad habit in business writing. It's usually done to create writing that sounds official and objective. It adds length without contributing additional meaning.

You'll often see nominalization in sentences that feature prepositional phrases and the passive voice. They're all part of the common impulse in business writing to make sentences longer so that they'll sound more authoritative. The cure for nominalization is to convert these phrases back to the original verb or adjective they came from.

Instead of

Heavy traffic on Monday morning **caused the network to experience slowness.**

Try

Heavy traffic on Monday morning **slowed the network down.**

("Experience slowness" is a nominalization of the verb "slow.")

Instead of

Engaging in regular discussion *about expectations can help* **enhance the performance** *of employees.*

Try

Discussing expectations *regularly can help employees* **perform** *better.*

("Engaging in discussion" is a nominalization of the verb "discuss"; "enhance the performance of" is a nominalization of "performing better.")

Most writers aren't even aware that they're using nominalizations; they're just trying to make their writing sound more "businesslike." Once you become aware of the pattern, it's easy to recognize it and to say what you mean in a clearer and more straightforward way.

4. Watch for padding

We've looked at how relying on the verb "to be" can make a sentence long and sloppy. We've looked at how prepositional phrases and nominalizations can make sentences unnecessarily long. Now let's look at padding—that is, using more words than you need.

There are lots of ways to pad a sentence. Two of the most common are using **redundancies** and relying on **filler words and phrases** that don't add meaning.

Redundancy in writing is unnecessary repetition. Here are some common redundancies that might look familiar to you:

10 a.m. in the morning ("a.m." means "in the morning")

Absolutely essential (if something is essential, it's essential; something can't be "sort of essential")

Advance warning (all warnings occur in advance)

Basic fundamentals (fundamentals are basic)

Current trend (unless you're writing about a historical trend)

Final conclusion (a conclusion is final)

Follow after ("follow" is enough)

Merge together ("merge" implies "together")

Group together ("grouping" is putting things together)

Future plans (all plans are for the future; you can't plan for the past)

Postpone till later ("postpone" means reschedule for later)

Still remains ("remains" implies "still")

Unintentional mistake (if it was a mistake, it was not intentional)

Some writers use redundancies as rhetorical devices, for emphasis.

Sales and marketing would like us to increase production to meet the spike in demand. But in actual fact, we cannot increase production that quickly, so we need to find a way to engage the market realistically given our current limited capacity.

In this example, "actual fact" is a redundancy (all facts are actual facts), but the writer has used this expression to emphasize his point that sales and marketing are asking for something that's not realistic.

Most of the time, though, writers use redundancies unconsciously. It's a bad habit you have to break.

An occasional redundancy isn't such a big deal, unless you're a real stickler. The problem comes when this kind of writing expands and becomes ingrained. This habit feeds into the tendency of some business writers to write unnecessarily long and needlessly complex sentences, trying to sound professional and authoritative. Consider a sentence like this:

Everybody must share a clear common understanding of the company's key risks and a clear line of sight into the overall general level of exposure to those risks.

You can see there's repetition in the sentence ("clear"), but there's also significant redundancy. When "everybody" has an understanding, it's already "shared." If it's a common understanding, then everybody has it. So the beginning of a revised version of this sentence might go something like this:

Everybody must share an understanding of the company's key risks . . .

What about "a clear line of sight"? Doesn't that just mean "understand"? And what's the difference between "overall" and "general"? Aren't they the same?

So how about this version instead:

Everybody must share an understanding of the company's key risks and its level of exposure to those risks.

You could even take it this far, if you wanted to trim more:

Everybody must understand the company's key risks and its level of exposure to them.

Let's look at another example:

The projected cost for the renovation is estimated at approximately $11 million.

"Projected," "is estimated," and "approximately" all convey the same idea. One alternative version of this sentence:

The projected cost for the renovation is $11 million.

Once you become attuned to redundancy in writing, you'll begin to see it everywhere, and you'll get better at stopping yourself from writing redundant prose. Your writing will be more concise and clearer, with a more natural voice.

Another problem that can make your writing bloated is the habit of using **filler words and phrases** that don't add meaning. Consider these overused words and phrases:

Actually	I just wanted to
A number of	In many cases
Apparently	In many ways
At the end of the day	Literally
A variety of	Meaningful
Basically	Significant
Completely	Totally
Currently	Very
Entire	Whole
Honestly	With reference to

Of course, all these terms have meanings, and when they're used precisely they contribute to the meaning of the sentence. The trouble is that they're often dropped thoughtlessly into sentences where they contribute no meaning at all.

In many ways, the cost estimate is higher than expected.

In *how many ways* was the estimate higher than expected? (How many ways *could* an estimate be higher than expected?) If there's no answer to this question, the phrase is probably serving no purpose except to take up space.

With reference to the proposed expansion, I really don't support this idea.

This sentence is awkward; getting rid of the filler can help:

I don't support the idea of expansion.

Here's another example:

Hi all,
I just wanted to check in about the whole video production process. I totally agree with Sam that it's very important to involve the full team at the kickoff meeting.
　　Felix

Felix's entire first sentence feels like padding. His real message is in fact very brief:

Hi all,
I agree with Sam that the whole team should be involved in the video kickoff meeting.
　　Thanks,
　　Felix

Sometimes people pad their writing for social reasons—they want to sound friendly or they don't want to sound abrupt. Consider if there are other ways to create a friendly tone in your communication, rather than padding your writing with meaningless phrases. In the second example above, the "Thanks" added to Felix's brief message creates goodwill with his readers. It might take a minute or two of thought, but you can be concise and polite at the same time.

Work with Drafts

It's likely that every English teacher you ever had told you to work through multiple drafts when you write. Maybe you did writing assignments in high school or college that included writing a rough draft, getting feedback from the instructor, and then rewriting the draft at least once. If you're like most people, when you started writing at work you realized you didn't have a lot of time to get your writing done, so the idea of working with drafts seems like an impossible luxury.

While you might not have as much time as you'd like to polish your writing, developing a sensible approach to working with drafts can improve your writing significantly and can save you time in the long run.

The reason working with drafts leads to better writing is that it allows for time between iterations. During this time, you develop a different perspective on what you've written, even if you're continuing to think about it (or perhaps because you're *not* continuing to think about it). That different perspective helps you catch errors, notice gaps in content, cut out extraneous information, and recognize that you might have said something insensitive or politically unwise. Getting that little bit of distance can help you take a more objective eye to your own writing.

So the trick is to build in some time between iterations, even during your busy workday. You probably won't have a week to let your first draft rest, but can you find a day between drafts? If not a day, how about a few hours? Some business writers do all their important writing for the day first thing in the morning, when they feel fresh, and then return to their drafts near the end of the day. The time that's passed during the workday lets them revisit and revise what they wrote in the morning.

If this kind of system won't work for you, do whatever you can to take a break after you write your first draft. For instance, try writing out a quick draft before you have to go into a meeting, and then checking it before you need to send it out. Try grabbing a cup of coffee between your first and second drafts. Do whatever you can within the confines of your busy day to help yourself get some distance on your early drafts and enable you to make improvements in later ones.

It can be difficult to find additional time in the day, but devising a system that allows you to work with drafts will save you time in the long run—your communications will be clearer and more complete, and you'll spend less time following up to clarify.

Writing Is Rewriting

Steve Strauss

Would you ever expect to go to the theater to watch a movie and see the director's very first cut or the raw footage of the film? Of course not. When you read a book, are you getting the author's unedited first take of the manuscript? Again, no. Why is that? Because we know that when someone has an important idea to convey—whether it is a director or an author or whoever—they will take the time to do it right and give us their best effort.

The same should be true for you and your business writing. Writing is rewriting (or it should be). It doesn't matter whether you are writing a blog, a letter, a proposal, or an e-mail. You owe it to your reader—and, more importantly, to yourself—to take the time and have it say what you really mean. And that requires some editing, plain and simple.

Very few of us can put down on paper (or screen!) exactly what we want to say the very first time we think it. Either the idea will be unformed, or it won't come out exactly as intended, or there will be typos. Whatever the case, it is vital, if you want your writing and ideas to be both understood and taken seriously, that you take a little extra time, give the item a little extra effort, and have it say precisely what you mean.

Ask yourself this question: What would you think of a job applicant whose cover letter got your address wrong, or contained typos, or used "i" instead of "I"? You would likely think that the person is lazy, sloppy, or uneducated—or all three. Yet that is the very risk you take when you don't edit, review, and rewrite your writing. Doing so will not only ensure that you avoid mistakes that can be damaging to your business, brand, or career but will also mean that the recipient will truly understand what it is you are trying to say.

That will happen, however, only if you live by the mantra "Writing is rewriting."

(And, by the way, I edited this sidebar eight times.)

Steve Strauss is a best-selling author and the senior USA Today *small business columnist. He runs the website TheSelfEmployed.com.*

STEP 5: FILL IN MISSING CONTENT; DELETE EXTRANEOUS CONTENT

"I hate it when I have to wade through a bunch of information I don't need to get to the information I do need."

—SURVEY RESPONDENT

Most of us are writing in a hurry, and one of the biggest risks of writing in a hurry is making mistakes with content—either forgetting something or including too much. When you write a first draft, you tend to just splat out whatever is in your head. Sometimes you include information that isn't really relevant. Sometimes you forget to include important content. That's perfectly normal for a first draft, but before you send your document off to its final destination, you need to be sure you've included the right content.

Forgetting important content usually has one of two possible outcomes. Either the reader zones out and gives up, or he has to follow up with you to get the content he needs, wasting time on both your parts.

Including too much information can also make life harder for your reader. Extraneous content will force your reader to work to figure out why you're saying all this and what she's supposed to do about it. If your message ends up being too long and vague, your reader might give up entirely.

A quick content check helps ensure that your readers are getting exactly what they need.

Let's look at a couple of examples to see how this works.

All,

Just a reminder that next Thursday's training session is mandatory. Everyone in the group needs to complete diversity training for compliance purposes.

If you haven't done the diversity training module during the last twelve months, you need to do it this time. Everyone has to complete the training by the end of May, or it could affect our licensing.

We've got two more slots with the vendor. Please ensure you make it to one of the two upcoming sessions. If you know you cannot make it, let me know now.

Thanks,

Mona

You can tell that Mona is concerned about making sure everyone gets this training and that she's worried about what will happen if people miss it. She's also worried that people are going to blow it off. She's so worried about these issues, she's forgotten to provide helpful information about when and where the training will take place. First she mentions "next Thursday," then she refers to "two more slots with the vendor," and the overall effect is confusing.

Mona takes a step back and thinks about what her readers really need, what's at stake, and how to communicate it best. She realizes that she needs to add those dates.

All,

To renew our licensing, everyone in the group must complete the diversity training module by May 31. If you haven't yet, you have two more chances:

February 11: 2–3 p.m.

March 27: 10–11 a.m.

If you don't remember the last time you did this training, let me know and I will confirm. If you absolutely can't make either of these times, let me know immediately. This has to get done.

Thank you!

Mona

Reviewing your draft for content often helps you improve it in other ways as well. Mona has added the new information her readers need—

the dates of the training sessions—and in the process of thinking it through, she's also managed to cut down the overall length of the message. Moreover, she has brought the issue of licensing to the very beginning of the message, letting her readers know what's at stake right away.

Including too much information can be as problematic as including too little. We often include too much because we're more focused on ourselves than on our reader. A quick review of a draft can help tighten up the communication.

Alec works for a regional bank that's about to launch a new customer service initiative that will include getting more customers into the Elite Checking program. Currently branch personnel are offering customers Standard Checking as a default. As a result, customers who qualify for the better account are missing out on rewards, and some are paying unnecessary fees. Alec drafts a memo to branch tellers and other personnel introducing the new initiative. Here's his first draft:

Hello MaxxBank AllStars!

I'm writing today to announce an exciting new initiative for MaxxBank: the EliteStar program. As part of the initiative, we have a goal to bring 20 percent more new customers into Elite Checking accounts, and to move 20 percent of existing customers from Standard Checking into Elite.

Based on research throughout the region, we estimate that currently about 30 percent of existing customers in Standard in fact qualify for Elite based on their running daily balances. And about 25 percent of new customers are placed into Standard Checking when they would be better served by Elite Checking. The result is that many of our customers are being underserved and missing out on the benefits that Elite offers. These customers often incur service charges that they would not be subject to if they had Elite status. We are managing a large volume of complaints across the branches as a result. We estimate that by moving qualified customers to Elite status, we can reduce fee-related complaints by as much as 35 percent. And the revenue from the lost fees could be offset through happier customers engaging with the bank in other ways, say, through credit cards, home loans, mortgages, or other products.

Over the next few weeks, we'll be rolling out training to make it easier for branch personnel to recognize potential Elite customers and help them have conversations to invite customers into the program. Keep your eyes open for more communication about this exciting initiative!

Alec puts his draft aside and comes back to review it the next day. Reading it over, he realizes that the content in the middle paragraph was on his mind because of a meeting he'd attended that day, but it really isn't helpful to his readers. It makes the memo too long and tedious to read. In fact, some of that content—the section about making up lost revenue—he would prefer *not* to share with the branch personnel, because he doesn't want to risk their passing it on to customers. That's information for internal consumption only. He does want to provide some explanation for the initiative, though, because people perform better when they understand why they're doing what they're doing.

Here's Alec's second draft:

Hello MaxxBank AllStars!
I'm writing today to announce an exciting new initiative for MaxxBank: the EliteStar program. As part of the initiative, we have a goal to bring 20 percent more new customers into Elite Checking accounts, and to move 20 percent of existing customers from Standard Checking into Elite.

Research shows that many of our Standard customers qualify for Elite status, and they're missing out on the great rewards they could be enjoying, including free checks, overdraft protection, and interest on their balance. We want to ensure that these customers get the most from their MaxxBank relationship!

Over the next few weeks, we'll be rolling out the EliteStar

training to help you identify potential Elite customers and bring them into the right account for them. Keep your eyes open for more communication about this exciting initiative!

In his revision, Alec removes the figures and some of the detailed rationale from the middle paragraph, and instead writes a middle paragraph with a clear message that will resonate with his readers: we're launching this initiative to make sure that customers are having the best possible experience with MaxxBank. In this case, less content makes for a more effective communication.

Use Structure to Help You Choose Your Content

Not everyone likes to use outlines when they write. If you're writing something very short and straightforward, an outline might be unnecessary. But sometimes with a longer document, structuring your message with a quick outline can help you make sure your content is complete and you're presenting it in a logical way. The outline doesn't have to be complex; it can be a list of topics, which you then arrange in the order in which you want to present them.

You can even outline after you've written a draft, to check whether you're including the appropriate information—and nothing extraneous. Outlining after the fact is called "reverse outlining." Let's look at reverse outlines of the two versions of Mona's message above.

Original version
* Diversity training is mandatory for compliance purposes.
* You have to go to the diversity training once during twelve months so we can get our licensing.

* If you haven't been to a session yet, you must go to one of the two remaining ones this year.
* Let me know if you have problems.

Revised version
* Everyone has to do this training or we won't get licensed again. Here are your chances.
* Here are the two dates of trainings.
* I'll help you make sure it gets done; let me know if you have problems.
* We have to do this.

You can see in the revision of Mona's message that she hasn't just added the missing information (the dates and times of the training sessions); she's also restructured her entire message to make it clearer to her readers.

Writing a quick outline doesn't have to be a big deal, but it can make a big difference in the content and quality of your message.

How to Get the Content Right

If you like to **plan** before you write, you should think about your content in light of the work you did for Step 1, *Get the ask clear*, and Step 2, *Write for your reader*. Ask yourself these questions:

What content must *I include to achieve my purpose in writing?*
What content does my reader need?

If you're the kind of writer who likes to create a first draft and then **edit**, make sure you do a content check as part of your revision process. Including extraneous content often comes from the writing equivalent of "thinking out loud"—mulling over or reviewing content in your own mind without considering if your audience needs it. Sometimes it's helpful to your thought process to write everything out. But if the content isn't useful to your reader, you should go back and cut it out. If you've already got a draft, take a quick pass over your document. Look at your pieces of information one at a time and run through a mental checklist:

Is this all the information my reader needs?
Does my reader really need this information?

Whether you're a **planner** or an **editor** by nature, taking a quick content inventory before you send your draft will help you meet your readers' needs.

SUMMARY: Fill in Missing Content; Delete Extraneous Content

* Think for a moment before you start to write or before you send: "What do I want my reader to do?"
* Then ask yourself, "Have I given them the information they need to do this? Have I given them content they don't need?"
* Organize and edit your draft with this in mind.

Now that you feel confident about your content, we'll explore how to write your message as clearly as possible.

STEP 6: WRITE IN PLAIN ENGLISH

"I find it frustrating to be somewhat trapped by a long-standing and robustly implemented 'institutional writing voice.' This enforced company style is overly wordy, full of run-on sentence structures and embraces a bureaucratic, impersonal tone that might be 'legally effective' but not effective in motivating or communicating with the audience. Ultimately the impersonality of the tone is off-putting to readers and can often be misunderstood as authoritative or even hostile."

—SURVEY RESPONDENT

Business writing is often mocked for its heavy reliance on jargon and unnecessarily convoluted language. Modern-day corporate-speak comes from a variety of sources outside the business world: from the military, from sports, and from law, among other fields, often driven by the latest trends in management thinking. As businesspeople became more interested in warfare analogies, the habit of using military-style acronyms and specialized vocabulary grew. As businesspeople began to envision themselves as athletes, sports metaphors crept in. And because there's always been a close connection between business and the law, some of the worst tendencies in business English come from aping legal writing—trying to sound authoritative and official, and muddying the meaning in the process.

The pushback against these tendencies started in the 1970s. The plain English movement arose in response to the ridiculously obscure legalistic writing in government documents. In 1977, New York State passed laws requiring plain English in consumer contracts and leases. In 1978, President Jimmy Carter issued two executive orders mandating that government regulations be easy to understand. There is similar legislation across the English-speaking world.

There are no laws against muddy, convoluted, jargon-ridden business writing, so it's up to us to fix it on our own. The good news is that you can distinguish yourself by saying what you mean in plain English.

Jargon

There are two kinds of jargon. One is the language specific to your business or industry: acronyms, abbreviations, and specialty vocabulary used as a shortcut among people who understand it:

> *Will the ASB be ready in time for SteerCo? If not, I suggest we prioritize the alpha of ITB so the team can review it prior to the launch of ELF.*

Almost everyone who has a job has written this way at one time or another, and most of the time it's perfectly fine. Sometimes, though, it's not. When you use heavy jargon outside your immediate work circle—among people who don't understand it—it can create a barrier to understanding. It can be a particular problem in proposals, where it can confuse, annoy, and alienate readers.

The other kind of jargon is that common group of business buzzwords and clichés that many of us desperately overuse (*moving the needle, circling back, drilling down*, and so forth). Using this kind of jargon excessively, even when your audience will understand it, can flatten your writing and diminish its impact. Relying too much on jargon can make you sound sloppy, as if you're not willing to do the work to express what you mean accurately.

How many of the phrases below do you see in a typical workweek?

Actionable	Blue-sky thinking
Aligning	Boiling the ocean
At the end of the day	Boots on the ground
Bandwidth	Deep dive
Best practice	Delta (instead of "change")

Disruptive	Reaching out
Game changer	Reality check
Going forward	Strategic
Hard-baked solution	Synergy
Impactful	Taking the pulse
Iterate	Thought shower
Leading-edge	Tools
Leverage	Touching base
Low-hanging fruit	2.0
Moving the ball forward	Upskill
No-regrets move	Value add
Popping the bubble	Warning shot
Quick win	

I'm sure you could add to the list. Such phrases are often metaphors, as you can see, and taken in bulk they're just comical. Things really get interesting when writers begin to mix these metaphors; the result is often pure nonsense:

Have you noticed that the farther you move toward fulfilling your potential, the higher the needle moves forward?

Wait, which way is the needle moving? Up or forward? It's a silly example, but it came from a real document, and it illustrates what happens when people rely on these expressions too much: they stop thinking. Consider how distinctive and refreshing your voice as a writer could be if you cut down on your use of this kind of jargon.

Instead of
Going forward, we should drill down into actionable initiatives rather than blue-sky thinking.

Try
In the future, we should focus on initiatives that we can actually implement rather than unproven ideas.

Instead of

> *At the end of the day, we can advance by targeting quick wins and low-hanging fruit in the market.*

Try

> *Ultimately, we'll succeed if we focus on easily achievable goals.*

You'll note that both of these examples do more than eliminate offending phrases. The revisions are more specific and easier to understand than the originals. They present concrete ideas that can be discussed and perhaps disagreed with. Do we really want to stick with what we already know how to do, without exploring other avenues? Is focusing on easy goals really the right thing to do now? When you strip these suggestions of their jargon, it becomes much easier to understand and discuss them.

Needlessly Complicated Language

In Step 4, *Be concise*, we looked at the bad habit of using long phrases where short ones would do. In that step, we were concerned about saving space and writing economically. Here we're concerned with a different issue: how using language that's needlessly complicated can instead impinge on your ability to communicate.

What do I mean by "needlessly complicated" language? Here are some examples:

Utilize = use	With regard to = about
Initiate = start	Regarding = about
Subsequent to = after	At this time = now
Prior to = before	At this point in time = now
In light of the fact that = because or since	By means of = by
In the event that = if	In accordance with = under, by
In close proximity = near	In order to = to
In the near future = soon	In the absence of = without
With reference to = about	In cases when = when

The basic pattern here is taking a small, simple word and replacing it with a bigger word or a series of words. Just as with jargon, the impulse behind this kind of writing seems to be that it will make you look smarter or more serious or more professional. Why merely *begin* something when you can *initiate* it? Why *use* a thing when you can *utilize* it?

You'll notice that a lot of these forms are prepositional phrases, which we discussed in Step 4, *Be concise*. Learning to recognize them is a useful tool in improving your writing skills.

This kind of deliberate complication is everywhere in business. It has seeped into customer service training. Cashiers in some stores have stopped calling for the "next" customer and started saying "following" instead, as if adding those syllables demonstrates superior customer service.

Of course, stores are not fooling customers about the quality of their service simply by having associates say "following" rather than "next." By the same token, you're not fooling anyone when you use needlessly complicated language in your writing. In fact, you'll impress people more if your writing is straightforward and clear. Let's look at some examples:

Instead of
> *In the absence of relevant performance data, we are unable to make an appropriate recommendation for an alternative software solution.*

Try
> *Without performance data, we cannot recommend alternative software.*

Instead of
> *In the event that you encounter a program error, utilize the indicated button on your screen to restart the program.*

Try
> *If the program crashes, click the Restart button.*

Instead of
> *At this point in time, we lack sufficient desk and seating arrangements to accommodate a full complement of staff in the office on a daily basis.*

Try
> *Right now, we don't have enough desks for everyone to come into the office every day.*

But Everybody Writes This Way

You might be wondering what the big deal is. Lots of people write this way—business writing just sounds like this. If everyone writes this way, then everyone will understand you, right? So what's the problem?

There are two problems, in fact. The first is that not everyone *will* understand you. It's possible to get your head so deeply into jargon and convoluted language that you're actually hard to understand. Look at this sentence, for example:

> *A strong risk identification process casts a broad net that captures all key risks and then drills down within the major risks to understand root causes.*

What?

Unless you're a risk consultant, you have to squint at this sentence pretty hard to understand what it's trying to say, which is this:

> *A strong risk identification process helps you understand the key risks and their causes.*

This "translation" might be too informal, but it captures the meaning of the original in much clearer terms.

The second problem with this kind of writing is that it can make you look bad. Ironically, most people start writing this way to sound smart. Then it takes over their brains. I've always felt that this habit made people look dumber, not smarter. It turns out I'm not the only one who feels this way, and there's research to support this conclusion. Carnegie Mellon psychologist Daniel Oppenheimer, in a paper called "Consequences of Erudite Vernacular Utilized Irrespective of Necessity: Problems with Using Long Words Needlessly," found that writers who use long words unnecessarily are perceived by readers as less intelligent than those who use simpler vocabulary.* In accepting the 2006 Ig Nobel Prize for Literature, Professor Oppenheimer explained, "It's important to point out that this research is not about problems with using long words but about using long words needlessly." He concluded: "One thing seems certain: write as simply and plainly as possible and it's more likely you'll be thought of as intelligent."†

Furthermore, I suspect that writing this way does more than make you *sound* dumb. I think it *makes* you dumber. I don't have any research to support this idea, but it seems to me that if you have a limited vocabulary, your thinking will be limited. If you have only a small set of ideas that your brain defaults to, can you really be "thinking outside the box"? I suppose it might happen the same way that relying on a GPS can short-circuit your sense of direction and prevent you from using your natural navigation skills. By accepting the challenge to write clearly, you'll challenge yourself to do better thinking.

When everyone else communicates this way, it's natural that you may want to fit in. Of course, there's vocabulary in any line of business, but there's also a voice, and we unconsciously adopt that voice. There's nothing wrong with fitting in; what's wrong is the "unconscious" part. So you fit in, and then eventually you sound like everyone else. But once you have some confidence, you might find the courage to start sounding like yourself. You will stand out in the organization if you have a distinctive and clear voice. It will be an asset to you. People will

* *Applied Cognitive Psychology* 20 (2006): 139–56; https://www.affiliateresources .org/pdf/ConsequencesErudite.pdf.
† "The Secret of Impressive Writing? Keep It Plain and Simple," https://www .sciencedaily.com/releases/2005/10/051031075447.htm.

see that your writing is clear and figure that your thinking must be clear, too. You don't have to write in businessese to sound smart. You'll sound even smarter if you can get rid of the jargon and the inflated language and write in a clear and direct voice.

Your Favorite Buzzwords

Everyone has favorite things: foods, clothing, movies . . . and language. You might find that you have particular buzzwords you use over and over again. I had a client once who couldn't get through the morning without calling something "foundational." He seemed to be completely unaware of how frequently he was leaning on the word.

What's the harm? For one thing, people notice it when you overuse buzzwords, and they will notice if there's one you tend to use repeatedly. For another thing, relying too much on one word can shape the way you think. A shortcut in communication can reflect a shortcut in thinking. When you default to repeating certain words, your vocabulary shrinks, and so does the way you perceive the world. Was everything my client noted really "foundational"? Sometimes he used the word to mean "seminal" (which is close to its actual meaning), sometimes to mean "original," and sometimes to mean "important." His overuse of the word had blurred the distinctions among the different meanings he ascribed to it, and his thinking, in this area at least, had become a little sloppy.

Is there a word you overuse? It's worthwhile noticing if you've developed an unconscious habit of depending too much on the same word. Breaking the habit can help you break into more specific and creative thinking patterns.

How to Write in Plain English

Breaking the habit of writing in businessese can be difficult. If you're a **planner** and like to outline your messages and documents before you start writing, you can use a trick that will make it easy for you to draft in plain English right from the start: explain the concept to your grandmother. This trick is very helpful in overcoming writer's block (see page 188), and it's also helpful when you want to express yourself in clear language. Your grandmother probably doesn't know what moving the needle means, and she'll probably laugh at you if you say you're going to initiate something rather than start it. Use your grandmother as a model audience to figure out how to say what you mean directly and without jargon.

If you're an **editor** and like to revise your drafts, you can also enlist the help of your grandmother. As you read what you've written, imagine that she's sitting next to you. Is there junk in your draft that would make her raise her eyebrows or shake her head? Get rid of it, and replace it with plain English.

Obviously you don't have to use your grandmother as this model reader—she's just a good example of someone who's probably intelligent and not overly impressed with fancy language. She's sympathetic to you and cares what you have to say, but she wants to understand it. You can choose any model reader you like—anyone who will help you get a different perspective on your writing, so that you can write more clearly.

Beware of Revision Fatigue

Every time you revise, you create the potential for new errors, and revising onscreen can increase this risk. Especially if you're working in a rush, it's easy to leave careless errors in your document. These are often the product of partial revisions:

> *I will be in the London next week.*

This writer initially wrote, "I will be in the U.K. next week," then decided to be more specific and say "London" instead. But she forgot to remove "the," and so ended up with this weird hybrid form.

Using tracked changes creates another risk: you might have a document so full of changes that you literally can't see what the final version will look like through all the strikethroughs and different colors of additions. So when you accept changes, you might inadvertently end up with something like this:

> *Tom Stevens and Karen Washington will lead consolidation efforts in the Midwest and regional strategy leadership and provide leadership in strategy in the region.*

With tracked changes showing, that revision looked fine, but with the changes accepted, it's clear that the actual editing wasn't quite finished.

Revision—especially when you go through many iterations—can cause fatigue and lead to errors. No matter how sick and tired your intensive work on the project has made you feel, be sure to go through your draft one last time before you finalize it to catch all the weird little errors that might have crept in. If you've been through so many revisions that you feel you can't "see" the document anymore, ask a colleague to take a quick pass through and clean up any clutter left behind.

SUMMARY: Write in Plain English

* Your writing will be clearer, easier to understand, and more effective if you write in plain English.
* Avoid excessive use of jargon, and avoid needlessly complicated language.
* To write in plainer English, imagine that you're writing for your grandmother or some other model reader outside the world of business. Express yourself clearly in a way that this model reader would understand.

STEP 7: IF SOMETHING FEELS WRONG, FIX IT

"So much aggravation and time-wasting could be avoided if people would just stop and think before they hit Send."
—SURVEY RESPONDENT

Ever finish a writing task and feel like there's something wrong? It could be an e-mail, or it could be something longer, like a proposal. It's not a great feeling, but it's also not uncommon. Most people who have this apprehension will struggle a little bit, maybe glance over their writing, fight back the feeling, and send the thing anyway. I'm going to suggest that you do not do that—that instead you spend a little more time figuring out what's bugging you and fix it, rather than sending something you're not confident about.

How? Let's look at a quick method for checking over your writing. First, run through Steps 1–6 quickly.

Step 1: Get the ask clear
Step 2: Write for your reader
Step 3: Start strong and specific
Step 4: Be concise
Step 5: Fill in missing content; delete extraneous content
Step 6: Write in plain English

Look especially closely at Steps 1 and 2—they're harder than they seem, and sometimes some extra attention to refining your purpose and writing for your reader will solve whatever problem you're facing. Step 5, *Fill in missing content; delete extraneous content,* is also worth special consideration. It's common to have afterthoughts about the information you're including. Have you said too much or too little?

What else might be bothering you?

Confidentiality

Maybe you're getting that nagging feeling because you're putting something in writing that you shouldn't. Are you including something that could make you or your company look bad? What if the content of your message or document became public? If that idea bothers you, you should probably revise what you've written.

Commitment

Are you overpromising? Are you committing to something you're not sure you can deliver? If you're making a commitment you're not sure you can meet, you should probably revise your message.

Politics

Does your document or message contain something that's politically unwise? Are you oversharing, about either yourself or someone else? Are you blaming someone when you shouldn't be? Are you aligning with someone you shouldn't or failing to align with someone you should? Political issues at work can be quite delicate, and if you've rushed through your writing, you might not have hit the right note the first time through. Take some time to consider your position and perhaps revise it.

Punctuation

Don't laugh. Who remembers the rules for comma usage? No one, that's who. Most of us have forgotten punctuation rules, if we ever learned them in the first place, and worries about punctuation can make otherwise good writers feel insecure about their writing. There's a very easy remedy for this: review the rules and be sure you're using punctuation correctly. Refer to the "Punctuation" section at the back of this book (starting on page 219) as often as you need to. Answering your punctuation questions can boost your confidence as a writer. Don't let punctuation bring you down.

Laziness

Laziness strikes even the most conscientious writers from time to time. Possible signs of laziness in your writing include lack of clarity and poor logical connections. Don't worry—this is precisely why we break the writing process into steps and work with drafts: to enable you to catch problems before you send them out into the world. Go back and put in a little extra effort to ensure that what you're sending is clear and complete.

Tone

Often when we feel that our writing "just doesn't sound right," the problem lies with the tone of what we've written. Most good everyday business writing uses a tone that's friendly and professional.

It's not always easy to get your tone right the first time. Two things, in particular, to consider are:

Your relationship with the reader
The importance of the topic (which includes what's at stake)

Checking your draft against these two points can help you correct an inappropriate tone.

The tone of business communication in most organizations is pretty casual, but not as casual as a personal chat. Check to make sure that what you've written is appropriate for work—no texting abbreviations, no super-casual expressions. (For more on tone, see "Does This Sound Okay?" on page 92.)

So, as you can see, there might be a number of causes behind that nagging feeling that there's something wrong with your draft. Let's consider some examples of messages that could be improved by one last review before they're sent out.

> Hi Terri,
>
> Would you mind sharing the Arris opening/closing titles used for the Arris conference as a .mov file with me? We have a couple more videos that popped up, and we're planning to handle these edits internally. Also, can you point me to a finished video as a model of the style we're looking for? I'm taking over from Sean on this project.
>
> BTW, the Walls files are now in the final folder on Dropbox.
>
> Thanks,
>
> Jared

Writing to Terri about Arris has reminded Jared that he also wanted to share the Walls files with her, so he drops in that information at the end of this message. This kind of last-minute addition is very common, and it's also very common for readers to overlook these afterthoughts. Mentioning an unrelated topic at the end of an e-mail on another subject creates a significant risk that the reader won't see it. It also makes it harder to organize and search e-mails by subject if the reader should want to go back later. In this case, it's better for Jared to send Terri a separate message about the Walls files.

Here's one that's trickier:

> Dear Ming,
>
> Please feel free to reach out to me directly if anything else comes up. David and Jon hadn't finished the analysis when they handed off the project to us, so David just had to contact me when you wrote to him yesterday. Amy and I tracked down the information you needed. There are likely other gaps, so please don't hesitate to contact me directly.
>
> Best,
>
> Brandon

Brandon's tone sounds a little snarky, and this first draft isn't as politically astute as it might be. Brandon is trying to tell Ming that David and Jon didn't finish the work, that he and Amy had to clear up their unfinished mess, and that she should not write to David for this information in the future. He's not happy about what happened, and he'd like to let Ming know that. However, when he reviews his draft, he realizes that he's throwing David and Jon under the bus and sounds passive-aggressive. He's uncomfortable with the first draft, so he revises it.

> Dear Ming,
> Please feel free to reach out to me directly if anything else comes up. I spoke with Amy yesterday while we were tracking down the information, and we both feel there might be other gaps. I'd be happy to find anything else you need.
>   Best,
>   Brandon

Brandon's revision gets the message across—that he and Amy did the work to find what Ming was looking for, that the project was not in fact completed, and that Brandon is the owner now—without explicitly blaming David and Jon. Brandon closes on a note of goodwill.

Here's one more first draft that felt wrong:

> Alison,
> Thanks for your message. We should be able to get those units out to your customer by June 2. I'll stay in touch.
>   Maria

Maria reviews her draft and feels a little worried. She realizes she's being vague and that she's not sharing with Alison what's really on her mind. She also realizes that her vagueness could lead to problems in the future, so she revises her message.

Alison,

Thanks for your message. I'll try my best to get those units out to your customer by June 2. However, we have two very large orders in the queue ahead of this request, so I am not sure we can deliver that quickly. Would your customer accept half the quantity by that date and the other half two weeks later? Let's talk about how to get this done. Please call me.

Maria

In her revision, Maria avoids the temptation to push the issue off her plate and explains what's worrying her. She briefly lays out the reason she might not be able to fulfill Alison's request and invites Alison to do some creative problem-solving with her.

Ask a Colleague for Input

If you're not sure what's bothering you, and you're working on something you don't mind sharing, ask a colleague to have a quick look at your draft. Whenever you ask someone for feedback on your writing, you'll get better results if you direct their attention to areas that concern you. It's fine if your question is simply "There's something bothering me about this draft; does it look okay to you?" But if you ask specific questions, you'll get more focused feedback. Try "Am I leaving out anything?" or "Am I approaching this right?" or "Am I saying too much?"

It's a great idea to find an informal proofreading and copyediting partner at work. You'll learn not just from your partner's comments on your writing, but also from looking closely at her work. You'll both become better writers.

Does This Sound Okay?

"Expressing the right tone is critical to avoid misunderstandings, without the benefit of facial expressions and body language."

—SURVEY RESPONDENT

Often when a piece of writing "just sounds wrong," there's a problem with tone. "Tone" in writing is like tone of voice. Your tone reflects your attitude toward the reader and toward the topic you're writing about. Your tone might be friendly, cordial, respectful, deferential, playful, abrupt, rude, or anything in between.

In business writing, appropriate tone can range from very informal—think of the website of an online grocery-delivery service—to very formal, such as communication from a bank. Most companies have adopted a tone that reflects their brand and their values, for both external and internal communication. The tone used in external communications—advertising, websites, messages to customers—will usually be the product of conscious, brand-driven decision-making. The tone used for internal communications usually develops more organically, with people emulating the style they see others using.

Several elements contribute to the tone of your writing. One of these is word choice: consider the different implications, for example, of "terrible," "very bad," and "not ideal." If your tone sounds harsh, you might want to replace some of your vocabulary selections with softer options. Consider the different impressions made by "awesome," "successful," and "impressive." If your tone feels too chatty, consider a more professional vocabulary.

Sentence length also shapes tone. Short, choppy sentences can sound abrupt. Long, complex sentences can come across as impersonal. Experiment until your writing sounds conversational but respectful.

Here are a couple of ideas about how to change your tone easily:

* Take the focus off the reader and put it on yourself:
  "You didn't send the information" versus "We haven't received the information"
* Consider whether deleting or changing a word or two can change your tone:
  "He still hasn't finished the analysis" versus "He hasn't finished the analysis"
  (The word "still" can suggest that he's missed a deadline or imply that he's a slacker.)
  "We expect to receive . . ." versus "We're looking forward to receiving . . ."
  ("We expect" sounds dictatorial; "we're looking forward to" sounds warm.)

It can be difficult to recognize the tone of your own writing. But if you're worried that your tone might not be appropriate, you might be right. If you're not sure you're hitting the right tone, ask a colleague to read over your draft and give you feedback on how it sounds.

Use Your Company's Style Guide

Many organizations that take written communication seriously have developed style guides for their employees to use. These guides vary a lot in length and scope, but the overall goal of all of them is to help ensure that everyone in the organization is communicating consistently.

Style guides serve a number of purposes. Like visual style guides, which specify the fonts, colors, and logos used in visual materials, written style guides can help keep an organization's branding consistent.

Style guides usually contain directions specific to your company. For instance, is it ever acceptable to abbreviate the name of the company in written correspondence, or should you always spell out its full name? What are the appropriate titles to use for people? Should those titles be capitalized? What are the correct names for products and services? How do you refer to the people who buy your products and services—are they "clients" or "customers"? Can you ever abbreviate clients' names in writing? This kind of information is especially important in situations where your company's public identity is in flux, such as during a merger or a rebranding.

Style guides also specify preferences in punctuation and spelling. Should you use the Oxford comma or not? (See page 219 for a definition of the Oxford comma.) Is it "Internet" or "internet"? Guides can also offer help with style issues—for instance, should you use "e.g." or "for example"?

Some style guides also provide reminders about basic grammar and usage. For example, when should you spell out numbers in text, and when is it okay to use numerals? When do you use double quotation marks, and when do you use single ones? How should you use a hyphen? These questions are especially important if your company is global and different rules apply across the different countries where the company operates.

It's worthwhile finding out if your company has a style guide—and, if it does, getting hold of it—when you're trying to put the finishing touches on your writing. Unless you're an editor at heart, you probably won't want to read your organization's style guide cover to cover, but you might find that it has the answer to that little question that's been bothering you. Using your company's style guide can help save you time and keep the brand voice consistent.

SUMMARY: If Something Feels Wrong, Fix It

* If something about your draft feels wrong, it probably is. Trust your gut.
* To help identify what's bothering you, try applying Steps 1–6 to your draft.
* Check your draft for problems around confidentiality, commitment, politics, punctuation, laziness, and tone.
* Consider asking a colleague to read over your draft and give you feedback.

The Checklist

Use this quick checklist either when you're writing or to check over something you've written.

THE SEVEN STEPS . . .

. . . to Success with Everything You Write at Work

1 **Get the Ask Clear**

Make sure you know why you're writing and what you're trying to achieve.

2 **Write for Your Reader**

Focus on what your reader needs and expects, not just on what you want. Make your writing appeal to your reader.

3 **Start Strong and Specific**

Craft an opening that makes your purpose clear and motivates your reader to keep reading.

4 **Be Concise**

Make your point as efficiently as possible.

5 **Fill In Missing Content; Delete Extraneous Content**

Do a quick content check to ensure that your readers are getting what they and nothing they don't need.

6 **Write in Plain English**

Business jargon can creep in unnoticed. Distinguish yourself by saying what you mean in plain English.

7 **If Something Feels Wrong, Fix It**

If you feel like there's something wrong with what you've just drafted, there probably is. Instead of sending something you feel uncomfortable with, take a minute to figure out what's wrong, and fix it.

The Checklist in Action: Before and After Examples

Now that we've looked at all the steps one by one, let's consider how you can use the entire checklist to improve your writing. We can start by reviewing some samples.

SAMPLE 1

Marie is working with two colleagues on developing a training program. She's received some feedback from a colleague on an early draft of the program, which includes some video animations. Marie writes a quick draft of an e-mail to pass along the feedback to her team.

Original

To: Francesca Wilson
CC: Kristoffer Hansen
Subject: Claudia's notes re animations
Hi,
Here are a few notes from Claudia's review of the training course that might have a bearing on the animations:

1. It should be "IRS," not "Internal Revenue" (not sure if we have this in the animations, but if we do, we should be consistent).

2. "Bn" or "billion"? (We use both.)

3. Should we number the parts of the framework? @Kris?

Ugh, will this ever end? Let me know what you think.
Thanks,
Marie

Checklist

Let's see how Marie applies the checklist to this draft.

1. GET THE ASK CLEAR

On reviewing the draft, Marie realizes that it's not really clear what she's asking Francesca and Kristoffer to do. She needs to fix that. She also realizes that if she shares her own opinions now, the team might resolve the problem faster.

2. WRITE FOR YOUR READER

Marie has two readers, but she's not asking the same thing of both. There's a special request for Kristoffer, only it's buried near the end of the message, where he might not see it if he's in a hurry.

3. START STRONG AND SPECIFIC

Probably because the ask isn't clear, the opening of the e-mail is mushy. Marie realizes that it will be easier for her readers if she spends a minute to organize the opening so they can skim it and understand what's required of them.

4. BE CONCISE

Marie thinks the draft is pretty straightforward and not too wordy. But she realizes that the two parenthetical expressions—"not sure if we have this in the animations, but if we do, we should be consistent" and "We use both"—are self-evident. They're a product of her "thinking aloud"—or in this case, "writing aloud"—and they can be deleted.

5. FILL IN MISSING CONTENT; DELETE EXTRANEOUS CONTENT

Marie recalls that there's an important deadline hanging around behind the scenes: if they want changes in the animation, they have to let the vendor know by Thursday, October 8, to stay on schedule. In her rush to pass along Claudia's comments, she's lost sight of this. She decides that this information belongs in the opening of the e-mail.

6. WRITE IN PLAIN ENGLISH

Marie determines that her draft isn't laden with jargon and is okay as it is. I agree.

7. IF SOMETHING FEELS WRONG, FIX IT

When she reads through the draft, Marie realizes that she's uncomfortable with her remark "Ugh, will this ever end?" She's sure her readers feel the same frustration, but on reflection the comment seems unprofessional, so she deletes it. If she's going to vent, it's better to do it in person.

Revision

To: Francesca Wilson, Kristoffer Hansen
Subject: Claudia's notes: decision needed by 10/7 for animations
Hi,
Claudia sent me the following notes on the training course that might have a bearing on the animations. My suggestions are in parentheses—let me know if you agree. **@Kris, we need you to answer #3**. We need to send any changes to VideoCraft by Thursday, 10/8, so **please get back to me with your comments by 10/7.**

1. It should be "IRS," not "Internal Revenue" (I'll check if this applies to the animations and make needed changes).
2. "Bn" or "billion"? (Let's use "billion" throughout.)

3. Should we number the parts of the framework? (I think no;
   why add complexity? @Kris?)

Take care,
Marie

Debrief

Marie used the checklist to create a much more effective draft, one that is not just a vague information dump but, rather, a communication that will move the project along. Francesca and Kristoffer will know from the very beginning what's being asked of them, by when, and Marie has given them some suggestions to respond to. She's called out the request for Kris, and she's also used bolding to draw attention to the asks in the message.

SAMPLE 2

Jeff works for a technology consulting company that's growing rapidly, and some clients have expressed worries that the firm is also consulting for their competitors. Jeff's company believes strongly that it can protect client confidentiality. Its legal counsel put together some advice for team leaders in evaluating potential conflicts of interest in staffing, and Jeff is assigned to convey this advice to senior management. Here's his first draft.

Original

The expectation is that with short, targeted, light-touch interactions with clients (e.g., discussion of tech trends or best practices, walk-throughs of the client's facility, outside-in diagnostics), our teams will not be conflicted from serving competitors. General guidance to team leaders is to delineate conflicts based on the role of the client staff member (and access to data). Ask yourself:

Does the staff member have access to confidential information? The criterion we apply in evaluating potential staffing conflicts is whether confidential information acquired by a staff member could materially disadvantage a client in serving another client.

Checklist

Jeff knows that he needs to improve this draft. Let's see where the checklist takes him.

1. GET THE ASK CLEAR

Jeff is asking his readers to understand the company's approach to potential conflicts of interest and to take action to comply with this approach. He feels that the ask isn't clear enough in the current version.

2. WRITE FOR YOUR READER

Jeff's original readers were supposed to be senior team leaders, but he realizes that the draft has wandered all over the place and it doesn't seem to be addressed to anyone at all. He'll think about his readers and adjust the content to meet their needs.

3. START STRONG AND SPECIFIC

This opening is passive, vague, and full of jargon; Jeff thinks it's more likely to drive readers away than draw them in. He also thinks the opening should make clear who this statement is for—who the intended readers are.

4. BE CONCISE

Oh boy. Jeff knows this draft is wordy and dense. He recognizes that the tone of the draft comes partly from his discussions with legal counsel. But the people he's writing for are not lawyers, they're managers, and they need more accessible advice.

But what exactly makes this draft feel too long and rambling? Jeff looks through the self-editing checklist:

Forms of the verb "to be"? Check. The first sentence is in the passive voice: "The expectation is." And the draft contains some of those floppy "is" phrases: "general guidance . . . is to" and "the criterion we apply . . . is." He can fix those.

Prepositional phrases? Jeff notes a number of prepositional phrases in the draft. Some seem okay, but others might signal places that could be condensed: "from serving competitors," "by a staff member" (there's another passive construction), "in serving another client."

5. FILL IN MISSING CONTENT; DELETE EXTRANEOUS CONTENT

It's pretty hard to tell at this point if the content is correct and complete. Jeff thinks it would be useful to provide a resource in case readers need further information.

6. WRITE IN PLAIN ENGLISH

Jeff sees some buzzwords that don't need to be there; he'd like to get rid of "light-touch," at least. And "criterion" seems unnecessarily formal—he'd rather be a little more conversational.

7. IF SOMETHING FEELS WRONG, FIX IT

The whole thing troubles Jeff, but he's especially bothered that no single point of view comes through. This draft is a pastiche of information he's gathered from legal and senior management. He wants to synthesize the information and write it in his own voice.

Revision

Senior team leaders should be aware of some general guidelines for preventing conflicts of interest when serving clients who are competitors. If we take the proper precautions, we expect that team members will not have a conflict of interest in serving competitors. To avoid such conflicts, team members' contact

with clients should be limited to short interactions such as
discussion of technology trends or best practices, walk-throughs
of the client's facility, and outside-in diagnostics. Team members
who have more substantial client contact should be assessed on
a case-by-case basis, determined by that team member's role
and access to data. A team member is likely to have a conflict of
interest if s/he has access to confidential information that could
be used to a competitor's material disadvantage. Any questions
about conflict of interest should go to Emily Jordan (ejordan@
tekxx.com).

Debrief

Jeff feels a lot better about this draft. Its purpose is clearer, it serves the
intended audience better, and it's written in a more straightforward
style. He's aware that this might not be the final version, but he'll circulate it among leadership and go through another draft or two.

Write It and Then Read It Out Loud
Barry Moltz

Most businesspeople who write articles or other long documents
type out their ideas on a laptop. They then typically go back and
revise what they wrote before they declare it finished. Unfortunately, even after revision, mistakes in spelling and grammar
often still remain in the draft when you try to edit it yourself.
Editing your own work is very difficult because you are so familiar with what you have written. When you reread, you have a
tendency to skip any mistakes you've made—they look "correct"
to you.

The best way to make sure that your document is correct is to
have another person edit it. Unfortunately, we don't always have

a copy editor available. When you do have to edit your own writing, the best approach is to reread the document out loud from the screen. Now, this might seem a bit silly or awkward, especially if there are other people around, but it really does work.

Carefully read the entire document out loud from beginning to end exactly as it is written. Make corrections in real time as you find mistakes. You might have to read the draft more than once to catch every error and every typo. Keep rereading it out loud from beginning to end until you find no more mistakes. Only then is the work complete, and you can feel confident that it's error-free.

Barry Moltz is a small business expert who gets companies growing again by unlocking their potential.

Types of Business Writing

This section provides specific guidance for different genres of business writing. It doesn't aim to be comprehensive. Rather, I've used input from the business writing survey I conducted for this book to confirm the kinds of things businesspeople write most often, and we'll focus on those. Here you'll find guidance on daily writing tasks, like e-mails and instant messages, as well as bigger tasks, like presentations and press releases. For all of them, you'll find prompts about how to apply some or all of the Seven Steps as you write and refine.

THE BASICS

E-mail

> "Bad e-mail is the bane of my life."
> —SURVEY RESPONDENT

Ask businesspeople what they do for a living, and you'll get all kinds of answers. Ask them what they do all day, and they're likely say, "Deal with e-mail." For most of us, e-mailing at work is as common as breathing. But it shouldn't be as thoughtless.

DO YOU REALLY WANT TO SEND AN E-MAIL?
It's easy to fire off an e-mail, but it's not always the right thing to do. Before you write, consider whether you really should (see the decision

tree in "To Write or Not to Write" on page 5). In some situations, you should definitely choose not to send an e-mail.

Don't send an e-mail when a phone call would work better. Endless rounds of e-mails to clarify, explain, and enlarge can often be prevented if you just pick up the phone.

Don't fire off an e-mail when you're angry. Give yourself time to cool off, so you don't send something you'll regret later.

Speaking of regret, if there's anything in your e-mail—anything at all—that might hurt you or your organization, don't do it. If you know or suspect that someone in your organization has done something illegal, unethical, unwise, or even just embarrassing, don't e-mail about it. E-mail is not private. It's discoverable in legal proceedings. Too many businesspeople are still far too careless about what they put in writing, and we see headlines about people incriminating themselves and their organizations in e-mails. There's no excuse. If you're not comfortable with reading about it on the front page of the *New York Times*, don't put it in writing. Pick up the phone instead, or discuss the issue face-to-face.

Make Sure Your Purpose Is Clear

If I could offer only one piece of advice for e-mails, this would be it: make sure your reader knows why you're writing. How many times have you plowed through a long e-mail trying to figure out what you're supposed to do with it? How many times have you given up on a long e-mail before you've fully understood what it's about? You don't want your message on the receiving end of this kind of treatment.

We're all moving fast when we compose and read e-mails, but it will actually save you time if you stop and think for a moment. Ask yourself, "What am I asking my reader to do?" The answer might be that you want your reader to take some kind of action. Or it might be that you want your reader to understand something. Whatever the answer is, put it into one sentence, and place a version of that sentence at the top of your message. You'll save your reader and yourself a lot of confusion and follow-up.

WRITE FOR YOUR READER

Consideration for your reader starts with your subject line, which should be concise and specific. A good subject line can help readers prioritize messages and find them later. If your message is especially important, consider putting "important" or "response needed" in the subject line. (See the box "Hints and Tips for Effective E-mails" on page 111 for more suggestions about effective subject lines.)

Think from the point of view of your reader as you plan and write your e-mail. Anticipate objections, and make it easy for your reader to reply.

START STRONG AND SPECIFIC

A recent study based on analytics derived from billions of e-mails suggests, surprisingly, that readers' attention spans seem to be increasing. Since 2011, the average time spent on reading an e-mail has grown by nearly 7 percent. That's the good news. The bad news is that even with this growth, the average amount of time spent on each e-mail is only eleven seconds.*

With slightly over ten seconds of reader attention, it's critical that you place your main point in the first three lines of your e-mail. If you count on your reader to scroll to the bottom of your message to get to the request, conclusion, or deadline, you risk losing him altogether.

GET YOUR CONTENT RIGHT

That short reader attention span also demands that you keep your message as brief as possible. Narrow down your content to the essentials, especially in an initial message. Follow-up messages can be longer, once you know that your reader is engaged.

You should limit each e-mail to one topic only. Secondary topics risk being buried at the bottom and never seen. The "one topic per e-mail"

---

* Chad S. White, "Email Attention Spans Increasing," Litmus Software, Inc., Company Blog, https://litmus.com/blog/email-attention-spans-increasing-infographic.

rule also makes it easier for you and your readers to search and find information in your in-boxes later.

FIX IT BEFORE YOU SEND IT

Before you send an e-mail, run though this quick checklist:

* Remember that e-mail isn't private. Don't put anything confidential in your message. If your e-mail contains anything that could incriminate or embarrass you, your colleagues, or your organization, delete it.
* Is there anyone you ought to copy? Do you really need to copy the people you are copying?
* If you're forwarding an e-mail, be sure there's nothing in it that you shouldn't share. Especially if you're forwarding a long thread, it's worthwhile scrolling down to check.
* Is it clear to your reader in the first couple of lines what you are asking of her?
* Have you made your message as concise as possible?

Get Your E-mails Opened and Read

"It is very frustrating when I find out that my e-mail was not read (completely), just glossed over. Then again, I do the same thing until I am ready to respond to the e-mail, and then I read it. But if no response is requested . . . or I'm not interested in the topic or discussion . . . I'll never know if a response was expected from me, because I haven't actually read the e-mail."

—SURVEY RESPONDENT

No one wants to send an e-mail that gets no reply. That has happened to all of us, and most of us have been guilty of failing to respond to a message we've received. When you send an e-mail, your message is competing with dozens, if not hundreds, of other messages in your reader's in-box. How do you craft a message that your reader will actually open and read?

It starts with the subject line.

* Make your subject line as specific as possible.
* Use the subject line to state the response required from the reader (e.g., "read only" or "response requested").

State your request within the first three lines of your message. Your opening should include:

* The context for the message and the request
* The request itself
* The deadline, if appropriate
* The recipient's incentive to continue to read to the bottom

Format your message for easy scanning.

* If your message is more than a few lines, use bullets and short paragraphs.
* Use bold to highlight deadlines and any milestones or intermediate deadlines.

Using these few simple tricks will make it easier for your reader to process and respond to your message. Over time, you'll develop a reputation as an efficient communicator who doesn't waste people's time, and you'll earn greater cooperation from your colleagues.

Hints and Tips for Effective E-mails
Patty Malenfant

In this day of short messages on Twitter and one-sentence captions on Facebook photos, the business world would do well to follow the same communication principles when using e-mail. To capture the interest of your reader so your e-mail will be read and you'll receive the response needed, you must communicate briefly and efficiently. Everyone's in-box is full, and you want *your* e-mail to be the one that gets read.

How do you do this? You need to use the e-mail subject line to state why you are sending the e-mail and what type of response you want. By inserting short action instructions before the subject, you can let the reader know what they need to do with your e-mail. Here are some examples:

* **READ ONLY:** This instruction lets the receiver know that the e-mail is just for their information; a response is not necessary, and no action is being requested. The receiver can hold this e-mail until a time in the near future to read it, but they do not have to act on it. Example: READ ONLY: ABC Client Accepts Proposal and Documents Being Finalized.

* **RESPONSE REQUIRED:** This instruction is for those e-mails where the receiver needs to do more than read—they need to reply. You are waiting for their response so you can take an action on your end. Example: RESPONSE REQUIRED: ABC Client Negotiated Contract Down $250.

* **ACTION REQUIRED:** This instruction lets the reader know that they need to do something with your e-mail beyond reading and responding—they need to take action. If you want to highlight a deadline for the action, you can add

"Deadline" plus that date at the end of the subject line. Example: ACTION REQUIRED: Contract Proposal Final Approvals—Deadline July 15.

✳ **EOM:** "EOM" stands for "End of Message." You will use this when you want to send only a quick message, comparable to a text message, but you are using e-mail. There is nothing in the body of the e-mail to review or requiring a response; in fact, there is nothing in the body of the e-mail at all, since the whole message is the subject line. Example: Wrapping up call—will be 15 minutes late for lunch EOM.

Now that you have mastered the subject line of your e-mail, you need to be sure the content in the body succinctly communicates to your reader what they must know and/or do. You will have no more than three short paragraphs of two to four sentences each. Introduce the e-mail with a professional greeting and close with the same before your name and title, as appropriate for your organization.

In the first paragraph, give your reader any background information they need to know. The second paragraph follows with the challenge at hand or what is needed. Use the closing paragraph to cover any remaining questions or comments about the follow-up required.

By following these easy tips, you can now go forth and be sure that your e-mail will be the one everyone wants to read!

Patty Malenfant is a human resources leader for a Fortune 500 hospitality company in the Washington, D.C., metropolitan area.

The Etiquette of E-mail Writing

Rosanne J. Thomas

Face-to-face communication is considered the best way to build relationships and deliver important messages. But the speed, convenience, and accuracy of text-based communication now make this mode the number one choice among professionals. We have a myriad of ways to communicate via text, but in business, e-mail is still the go-to method. However, there is a lot at stake with this mode of communication. Professionals at the highest levels have suffered extreme personal, financial, and health consequences as a result of carelessly crafted, hastily sent e-mails. And, of course, e-mail lives forever. How can we protect our reputations while maximizing the benefit of e-mail communication? Here are some guidelines.

* **Apply the standard of "if you would not say it face-to-face, do not write it in an e-mail."** Studies show that people are much "braver" when communicating from behind a screen and that the lack of nonverbal cues often makes e-mails sound more aggressive than intended.
* **Direct your message properly.** Double-check e-mail addresses. Do not send "Reply All" messages unless absolutely necessary. Use "BCC" (blind carbon copy) ethically, and not to mislead your primary recipient into thinking that the e-mail exchange is confidential.
* **Read through e-mail threads completely before responding or forwarding.** Use greater formality in e-mail composition with clients, company executives, persons from other cultures, and those you do not know well. Include an appropriate salutation and closing. Make sure sentences

are properly structured. Observe the rules of capitalization and punctuation.

* **Allow words to convey their meaning and emotion.** Steer clear of emoticons and emojis in professional e-mails. Avoid using all capital letters, no capital letters, multiple exclamation points, bold typeface, bright colors, or flashing text.

* **Proofread all e-mails.** Use but do not rely solely upon grammar-check and spell-check tools. Read e-mails aloud to be sure they reflect your intended tone.

* **Respond to e-mails promptly.** If you cannot respond at least by the end of the day, have an "Out of Office" message automatically sent back to the recipient. This will help preserve the relationship.

Rosanne J. Thomas is the founder and president of Protocol Advisors, Inc., of Boston, Massachusetts, and the author of Excuse Me: The Survival Guide to Modern Business Etiquette *(AMACOM, 2017).*

Requests

Most communications in business are requests of one kind or another. Whether you're asking for help or just for a bit of the reader's attention, taking the time to plan and craft your request—rather than winging it—can significantly increase your chances of getting what you want and can save you time and hassle over the long run.

What Do You Want?

The fundamental purpose of any request—be it for assistance, information, or any other goal—is to enlist the cooperation of the reader. In order to do that, you need to be very clear about what you're asking. This point sounds ridiculously simplistic, until you consider the number of messages you've received that have left you wondering, "What exactly do you want from me?" Unless your request is very straight-forward, it's worth taking a minute to clarify it in your own mind. If you're asking for help, is it clear what kind of help you want? What, specifically, would you like the reader to do, and when?

WRITE FOR YOUR READER

Understanding your objective and stating it clearly is only half of the communication equation. The other half is understanding your reader: her potential attitude toward your request and what it might take for her to say yes. If you can anticipate her response, you can address any potential objections she might raise and motivate her to respond positively to your request.

START STRONG AND SPECIFIC

You should state your request early in your message, to orient the reader and allow her to decide whether to read your message now or wait until she can give it more time and attention.

GET YOUR CONTENT RIGHT

In addition to being clear about your request, you should be sure to provide any information your reader might need to make a decision. Include any necessary documentation related to your request. Let the reader know how you prefer to be contacted, if it's not apparent.

Explaining the reason behind the request might help your reader respond favorably. Letting the reader know how important the request is to you can also motivate her to respond. How will you benefit if she grants your request? How might she benefit?

Your request should also include a deadline, if applicable and appropriate. Be sure your deadline is specific—asking for a response "ASAP" makes it easy for your reader to forget about your request. If you have a particularly tight deadline, explain the reason behind it. People will work harder to meet a deadline if they understand the reason for it.

CHECK IT BEFORE YOU SEND IT

Before you send off your request, check it over to make sure nothing feels wrong:

* Make sure your request comes early in your message and is clearly understandable to the reader.
* Use a courteous, not demanding, tone. Remember, you're trying to gain cooperation from your reader.
* Don't take your reader or his attitude for granted, and don't assume he'll say yes to your request.
* Remember to thank your reader.

SAMPLE E-MAIL WITH A REQUEST

To: John Mottola
Date: April 17, 2019
Subject: Can you share configuration for BBL?
Hi Jack,

I'm writing a proposal for Evergreen, and I'm wondering if you could share the details of how you configured the package for the BBL installation. I'd like to do something similar for Evergreen. I want to submit the proposal on April 26.

I looked on the CRM, but I don't see a lot of detail there. Can you shoot me an e-mail or spend a few minutes on the phone with me?

Thank you!

Kelby

Escalated Request When a Deadline Is Approaching

When a deadline is looming and you haven't had the response to your request you need, it's time to escalate. An escalated request follows the same basic principles as an initial request, but it's pared down to the essentials and it makes a special appeal to the reader.

* Edit the subject line. When you send a follow-up to your request, edit the subject line to let the reader know the deadline is looming. If your original subject line was "Can you provide data for the report?," you might edit it to say "Deadline Friday: Can you provide data for the report?" or "Reminder: Can you provide data for the report?"
* Keep it short. Your follow-up request should be brief and should contain the most essential information the reader needs to carry out what's being asked. Don't get bogged down in details.
* Acknowledge that the reader is busy.
* Let the reader know why the request is important to you or to the organization.
* Let the reader know why you're asking him and not someone else—what can he do that no one else can do for you?
* Restate the deadline, and explain why it's important.
* Offer to help. If there's any way you can make it easier for the reader, offer to do so.
* If appropriate, indicate that you'll follow up again shortly, maybe with a phone call.
* Be sure to say "thank you."

SAMPLE E-MAIL WITH AN ESCALATED REQUEST

To: John Mottola

Date: April 23, 2019

Subject: Deadline Friday: Can you share configuration for BBL?

Hi Jack,

Just following up on this. I'd like to use the same configuration you used for BBL in my proposal to Evergreen, which is due on Friday the 26th. I know you're swamped with JWB right now, but your insight here could really help us close the deal. Even just the server information would make a big difference.

I'll give you a call tomorrow.

Thank you for your help!

Kelby

Bad News Messages

Good news messages are easy to write, but conveying bad news can be rough. The key here is to save the reader's feelings to the greatest extent possible. That means opening with a buffer—a thank-you, if appropriate, or some kind of statement of appreciation. To avoid giving the reader false hope, though, you should transition very quickly to a diplomatic and kind statement of the bad news. If appropriate, it's fine to express regret over the news, but not an apology. If there's some hope of good news in the future, make sure you communicate that hope conservatively, without making a firm commitment. Close with a statement of goodwill.

> Dear Erik,
> Thank you for submitting the proposal for creating a task force on recruiting. You suggested some great ideas, but unfortunately we have to prioritize expanding the product line this season and we don't have the resources right now.
> I would like to return to this idea once we have the product line resolved. Let's stay in touch about it.
> Thanks again,
> Mack

Instant Messages

Instant messaging or chatting is nearly as quick and easy as talking, but it isn't talking—it's writing, and it requires a little care. No matter what IM or chat app you're using, these guidelines can help make your messages more productive and efficient.

Is IM the Right Medium?

IM is almost too easy to use. It's the default medium of communication for a lot of us at work, but it's not always the most appropriate one.

Before you ping a colleague, it's a good idea to slow down long enough to ask yourself a few questions: "Do I really need this answer immediately? Is it worth interrupting my colleague to get it in this way? Would it be more efficient to save up a few questions and ask them all at once? Would it be better to let my colleague answer in his own time instead of insisting on a response now?" It's also worth considering what kind of record, if any, you'll need of the discussion with your colleague. Some messaging programs preserve your message history when you shut down your computer, but others don't. So if you want an easily accessible record of your exchange, instant messaging might not be the best choice of medium.

Mind Your Manners

Respect the availability status of your colleagues, and if it's red, don't send a message unless it's an absolute emergency. Your colleague might be in the middle of a Webex or videoconference and not appreciate the distraction on the screen, or she might be concentrating on finishing a task.

You also need to be aware of tone when you're sending messages. It's easy to slip into a very casual tone. That's fine when you and your colleague are on the same wavelength, but take care you don't use a super-casual tone with someone you don't know well. Be especially careful if you have more than one chat window or channel going at once.

Remember that you're at work. Instant messaging can be fun, but you're not on Facebook or Instagram. Respect your colleagues' time, and exercise restraint when sharing to group chats or channels; remember that everyone is trying to get their work done.

Watch What You Say

Even when you're pinging with good work friends, remember that instant messages are official business communications. They are not confidential. They're the property of your company, and many companies monitor them. You're probably cautious about cursing in the office; you should exercise the same caution when you're messaging. One popular instant messaging program warns users: "Keep your conversations limited to what can be safely said in an elevator or a crowded restaurant." Keep it appropriate.

Using Instant Messaging Efficiently

A few little tricks can help improve the efficiency of your instant messaging. Before you launch into a long message, ask your colleague if she's there and available. Make your "Are you there?" message more specific by letting your colleague know what you want to ping about. Instead of "Hey, got a second?" try "Hey, got a second to review the XYZ agreement?" or "Hey, got a second to read something for me?" or "Hey, got a second to show me how to use that software?" And be frank about what you're asking for; don't type "qq?" if what you really want is to discuss whether or not to fire a vendor or some other large topic.

Presentations

Thirty million PowerPoint presentations are given every day throughout the world. How can you make yours memorable?

Pinpoint Your Purpose

Attention can wander during a presentation, so it's important that you know exactly what you want to get from yours. As an exercise, try creating a one-sentence objective for the presentation, such as "By the end of the presentation, I want the audience to understand that our solution offers more tools than the competition's does and can be customized for their needs" or "By the end of the presentation, I want x members of the audience to request an onsite demo" or "By the end of the presentation, I want to have cleared the obstacles to partnering on this project." Try to make your objective as active as possible, in order to avoid building a presentation that's essentially an information dump. What do you want your audience to *do* as a result of seeing your presentation?

WRITE FOR YOUR AUDIENCE

As you work on your slides, think from the point of view of the people who will have to look at them. What are they expecting from your presentation? What information do they need? How would you feel sitting through this presentation? How can you make the slides easy for the audience to read and ensure that they reinforce your main points? Let your understanding of your audience's needs guide the preparation of your slides.

ORIENT YOUR AUDIENCE AT THE BEGINNING

The opening of your presentation is an especially critical moment. Presumably you have everyone's attention at the beginning. No one has had a chance to get bored, to get distracted by their phone, or to grow worried about the work they're not getting done because they're sitting in this presentation. Use this moment to let your audience know what will be covered in the presentation. Insert an outline slide at the beginning, and return to it throughout the presentation to help your audience with transitions and help them pace themselves in terms of energy and attention.

GET YOUR CONTENT RIGHT

There's a strong impulse when you're preparing your slides to include too much content. Research has shown that people typically remember only four slides from a twenty-page deck.* That's not very encouraging news if you're putting your heart and soul into an informative presentation, but from a strategic point of view, it's good to know. Rather than packing your presentation full of facts, you're better off choosing a few key points you want your audience to remember, and organizing the presentation around those. Think of your PowerPoint deck as a set

---

* Rexi Media, "How Much Do People Really Remember from a Presentation?," *Rexi Blog,* October 14, 2014, http://www.reximedia.com/how-much-do-people -really-remember-from-a-presentation/#.WbXlN9OGPxs.

of prompts for your performance rather than as a repository for complete information.*

Set up your slides as a visual aid for when you're making a speech or presentation, not as a trove of data. When presented with a very text-heavy slide, people will typically space out or stop listening and read the slide (people can read faster than you can talk). If you want to provide detailed information to your audience, you can make and distribute a leave-behind deck that contains your entire talk. For the presentation itself, keep your slides concise and the focus on you.

USE VISUALS EFFECTIVELY

Think visually as you create your slides.† There's no need to convey information only through words—think about how you can use images and graphics to get your points across. But be careful with graphs and charts: don't present graphics that are too small or detailed for the audience to see easily or understand quickly. If you have an important chart or table that is complex, present a simplified version of it on your slide and give the audience the full version, printed on paper, to examine more closely.

IF SOMETHING FEELS WRONG, FIX IT

Proofread your slides very carefully. Noticing a typo for the first time when you're standing in front of a group is a ghastly experience, and it makes you look bad. If possible, ask someone who is not familiar with the content to proof the presentation for you.

Allow yourself time to rehearse the presentation and revise it, even if you feel pretty comfortable about the content. Notice transitions

---

* Of course, there are different uses for PowerPoint. Some consulting organizations, for example, use PowerPoint decks to convey extensive data and recommendations to their clients, rather than as frameworks for oral presentations. In this section, I'm assuming you are using PowerPoint as a basis for a spoken presentation.

† A great resource for presenting ideas visually is Gene Zelazny's book *Say It with Presentations: How to Design and Deliver Successful Business Presentations* (New York: McGraw-Hill, 2006).

that aren't smooth, areas where your content seems thin, sections that drag. Rehearsing can give you more confidence and will improve your audience's experience by helping you improve your slides.

SLIDE REVISION CHECKLIST

* Choose readable fonts, and limit the number of fonts you use. Stick to a few basic, easy-to-read fonts, no more than two different fonts per slide.
* Use animation and sound sparingly and only if they support the message of your presentation. If they enhance the meaning and clarity of your presentation, use them. If they compete with your content, don't.
* In bullet points, use parallel grammatical constructions to help your audience follow your ideas.
* Use formatting like bold and italics sparingly and consistently. Too much of this kind of formatting can make your slides hard to read.

For sample presentations, please visit me at www.howtowrite anything.com.

Creating Visuals

Not all business communication occurs through writing—a lot occurs through visuals. In fact, words aren't always your best tool. Sometimes data is easier to understand if it's represented graphically. You don't have to be a graphic designer to learn the language of visual communication.

CHOOSE THE RIGHT GRAPHIC

There are lots of graphics options for you to choose from: photos and other images, as well as different kinds of charts and graphs. The type of graphic you choose will depend on your data and the story you want to tell with it.

COLUMN CHART

A column chart lets you compare values using vertical bars.

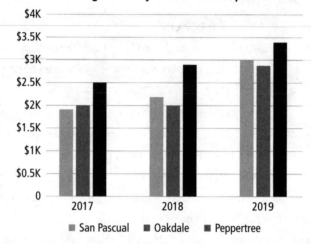

BAR CHART

A bar chart lets you compare values using horizontal bars. The layout of a bar chart makes it better suited than a column chart for data with long labels.

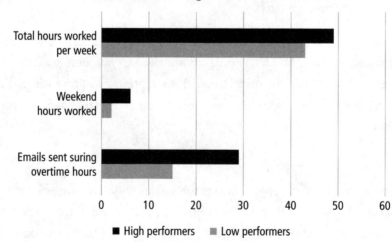

A stacked bar chart breaks out the components of a total number, so you can compare segments as well as totals.

Training Modalities across Performance Levels by Hours per Month

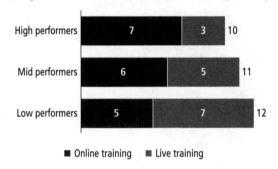

A line chart is used to track and compare values over time. It can show small increments of time more effectively than a bar chart can.

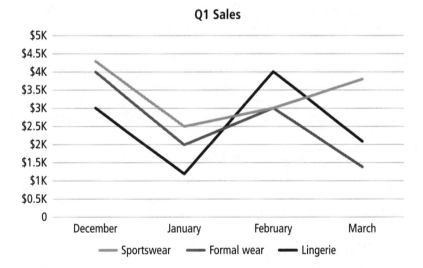

PIE CHART

A pie chart is a circle divided into slices, useful for showing numerical proportion.

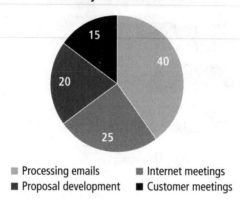

Weekly Task Allocation

■ Processing emails ■ Internet meetings
■ Proposal development ■ Customer meetings

DOT OR SCATTER PLOT

A dot or scatter plot shows data positioned on vertical and horizontal axes. It might be used to show the effect of one variable on another. In this example, a company is using a scatter plot to evaluate its competitors on two dimensions: geographic reach and scope of product offerings.

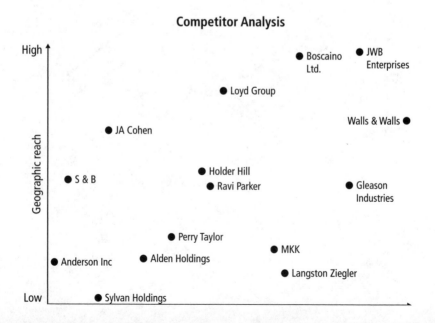

Competitor Analysis

Waterfall charts show how the cumulative effects of different inputs contribute to a net value.

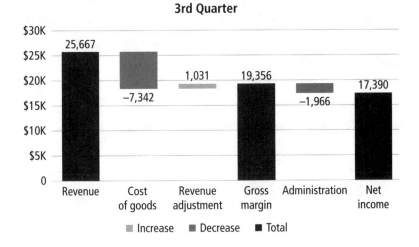

3rd Quarter

Funnel charts are often used in sales to show the potential revenue for each stage in the sales process. They can help you identify areas in the process where value is at greatest risk of being lost, and they can help identify an unhealthy sales funnel. In this example, the qualification process is not weeding out many prospects, which leads to many rejected proposals.

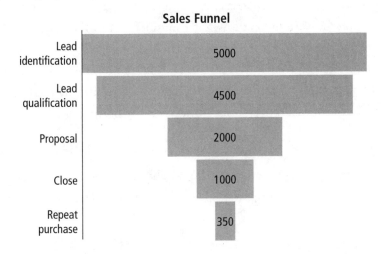

Sales Funnel

Make Sure Your Words and Graphics Complement Each Other

When you use words and graphics together, you need to make sure they work together in harmony and support each other. The first and most obvious rule is that the content of your words and graphics should be consistent. For example, if you're calling out some numbers from a graphic, make sure those numbers are accurate.

Avoid repeating the content of the graphic in your prose. If you're simply going to rehash the contents of the graphic in writing, there's not much point in including the graphic. Instead, strategically use information from your graphics to support the arguments you're making in prose.

Proposals

Businesses of all kinds create proposals for potential customers and clients—for example, to bid for work, to outline the scope of a job, or to state a price. The content of a sales proposal will vary widely, depending on the kind of business you're in, and most businesses have a standard format they use. Check to see if your organization has a proposal template, then use these suggestions to make it as compelling as possible.

Get the Ask Clear

If you write a lot of proposals, it's tempting to go on automatic pilot, filling in the various sections with numbers and other details. That approach is probably fine a lot of the time, especially if you provide the same service or product over and over. But it's worth mentioning here that you should pay attention to your prospective customer, and make sure your proposal reflects your understanding of their needs.

Write for Your Reader

If you're preparing a proposal, it's probably at the request of someone you've talked to at your potential customer. Needless to say, you should consider carefully all the information your contact has given you. You should also go beyond that. Depending on the situation, it's very likely that others in the organization will review your proposal. Who might they be, and what might they be concerned about? If your contact person is not the decision-maker, it might be worthwhile to ask who else will review the proposal.

Everyone reviewing a proposal will be concerned about cost, but don't assume that cost is the only factor. Really think about your reader's needs, and ensure that your proposal addresses them.

GET THE CONTENT RIGHT

Decide how you want to present estimates in your proposal. Sometimes estimates are binding. In other cases, the proposal contains a clause stating that the final cost may vary depending on a variety of circumstances. You should date your proposal and include an expiration date for the price quoted, so that you don't bind yourself to a price forever and there's no misunderstanding with the customer.

If there's a risk of cost overruns, address that risk directly and outline the factors that might cause them, including unanticipated circumstances on the job or changes in the customer's requirements.

If you feel the customer isn't entirely sure what they want, consider providing several different estimates for different options. Some companies routinely include add-ons in proposals, which can lead to more business, but add-ons can also annoy customers if they feel they are being upsold. Any add-ons you suggest should clearly address the customer's needs as you understand them.

CHECK IT BEFORE YOU SEND IT

If you're using a template for your proposal or repurposing a proposal you've used before, have a look before you send it to make sure you're including complete information and that you're not inadvertently leaving in the details of previous proposals, including the names of other companies and prices for other jobs.

Also check to see that you've included everything, and that your numbers add up accurately. Errors can be embarrassing and sometimes costly.

For sample proposals, please visit me at www.howtowriteanything.com.

RFPs

Some organizations will prepare and circulate a Request for Proposals (RFP) in search of a vendor to do a particular job, usually for jobs of a significant size. Some organizations that use public money are mandated to use an RFP in the bidding process.

If you're responding to an RFP, be very sure you follow its requirements exactly. Any deviation can throw you out of the running without further consideration.

A long sales proposal in response to an RFP may include the following elements:

Letter of transmittal	Equipment requirements
Title page	Cost analysis
Executive summary	Delivery schedule
Description of current problem	Summary of benefits
Description of current method	Breakdown of responsibilities
Description of proposed method	Description of vendor, including team bios
Analytical comparison of current and proposed methods	Vendor's promotional literature
	Contract

BUSINESS RELATIONSHIPS

Introductions

Providing written introductions for colleagues and associates is a vital part of business networking. A good introduction can get the dialogue started in a productive way.

Before we go any further, a note of caution: don't make an introduction if you're uncomfortable about doing so. An introduction is a kind of recommendation: you're essentially saying, "This person will be worth your time to talk to." Don't put your reputation on the line if you have any doubts about either party.

BE CLEAR ABOUT WHAT YOU'RE ASKING

When you introduce two people, it's your responsibility to set up the relationship. You should make it clear not just who the parties are, but why you're making the introduction in the first place.

Often the introduction will be of more benefit to one party than the other. Perhaps someone would like to do an informational interview, asking for information about a business or an industry or seeking career advice. When that's the case, be honest about it, and be sure you thank the party who (you hope) will provide the help.

CONSIDER BOTH OF YOUR READERS

Before you write the introduction, it's important to get permission from both of the parties involved, especially if you feel that either might be uncomfortable or unwilling. If someone has asked you to make the introduction, be sure you understand what they're hoping to get from the new relationship. Particularly when you're requesting a favor from someone, ascertain that they're willing to provide it before you put them on the spot with an introductory e-mail. Contact both parties separately to assess the level of interest and request permission to make the introduction.

Start Strong

Address both readers in your salutation. It's usually wise to place the name of the senior or more powerful person first.

Start by orienting both readers. Say explicitly that you're making an introduction, and explain why. Even though you've contacted both parties before writing the e-mail, remember that your readers don't know each other and will need to be reminded about the reason for the introduction. Mention how you met each of the parties, if that seems relevant.

Get Your Content Right

In most cases, your introduction doesn't have to be long. Offer a bit of information about both of the parties being introduced. In a quick e-mail, just a sentence can be enough. Suggest how this new connection might benefit each person. However, if it is clear that one party will benefit far more than the other, be straightforward about that, and thank the person who's granting the favor. If you are introducing a recent graduate to an executive, for instance, it is clear that the introduction will likely have greater business benefit to the younger person.

If you want to provide background information about either party, consider including a bio or a link to that person's website.

Finally, leave it up to your readers to decide on the next steps. Don't say anything to suggest that either of your readers is obliged to go forward with a meeting. Make the introduction and allow them to determine how to proceed. Don't offer to make arrangements for a meeting unless you're already sure that both parties are on board and comfortable with your playing this role.

Dear Louise, dear Su,

It's my pleasure to introduce you two. Louise, Su is the UCLA graduate I mentioned who is hoping to learn more about the analytics field—thank you for agreeing to speak with him. Su,

Louise has been working for Simons for nearly twenty years and can give you the best possible guidance on the field.

I think you'll enjoy knowing each other.

All the best,

Jill

Recommendations

Written recommendations are requested in a lot of situations: for college or graduate school, for other kinds of educational programs, for scholarships, and sometimes for employment purposes.

Think carefully if you're asked to provide a recommendation. Writing a letter of recommendation is a serious responsibility. You should never agree to write a letter of recommendation for someone who's unqualified, someone you don't really know, or someone you feel uncomfortable about supporting for any reason. It's better for you and the candidate if you say no than if you send out a lukewarm or vague recommendation. In addition, composing a good recommendation requires a significant investment of time and energy, so be sure you're ready for the task, and give yourself plenty of time to go through several drafts.

UNDERSTAND YOUR PURPOSE AND YOUR READER

It's easy to slip into generalities and platitudes when you're writing a recommendation. The cure for this risk is keeping a close eye on your purpose and your reader. Find out as much as you can about the opportunity the candidate is applying for, and focus your efforts on describing the fitness of the candidate for that role.

Put yourself in your reader's position. What will she be expecting to hear from you? What will she hope to hear? What information can you supply that will make her want to accept the applicant? What can you say to make her understand what's special about the candidate?

START STRONG AND SPECIFIC

The opening of your recommendation is important. You should announce at the very beginning of your letter who you're writing for, and for what purpose. Explain how you know the candidate and how long you've known him. State explicitly that you recommend the candidate.

Your first paragraph should express how strong your support for the candidate is. If you recommend him for the role, say so. If you offer your strongest possible support for the candidate, say that. If you cannot think of anyone better suited for the position, go ahead and state that here. Be honest about your degree of support, and don't make the reader persevere all the way to the end of the letter to learn how strongly you feel about the candidate.

GET YOUR CONTENT RIGHT

As you think about your content, confirm that you have complete information. Be sure that you understand the opportunity the candidate is applying for. If you feel fuzzy about it, find a website that can fill in the gaps in your understanding. It's also important that you understand what the candidate hopes to accomplish in the new program, initiative, or position. If you have questions about this, follow up with the candidate and get more details about his plans and aspirations. Get a copy of his résumé, so that your comments will be consistent with the information there.

What's really valuable about your recommendation are your personal and professional insights into the candidate and his abilities. Your letter can testify for the candidate in a way that his résumé or class transcript cannot. What you know about the candidate, and how that information fits into the bigger picture of the opportunity, is the core of your content.

Think about the special things you can tell the reader about the candidate that the rest of his record may not demonstrate. Think about what the new environment will demand of the candidate, and provide details that indicate he'll do well in that setting. Be specific and analytical about his qualities and accomplishments; don't rely on vague praise.

You may have been asked some specific questions in the request for a recommendation—for instance, as part of an application packet. Make sure your letter addresses those questions directly. If you've been asked about the candidate's weaknesses, don't ignore them. If you're grappling with a question about the candidate's shortcomings, write about a weakness that can be overcome. Better yet, describe how the candidate is already overcoming it. Consider whether the opportunity the candidate is applying for might be the perfect setting for him to address an area of weakness, and how he might perform.

FIX IT BEFORE YOU SEND IT

It's very likely that your first draft will be too long, and it may be unfocused. That's to be expected. Go ahead and write everything out, then take a break from it if you can. You might have received instructions about the desired length of the letter; don't go beyond that length, and even if there is no length restriction, don't exceed two pages. Keeping the length under control will force you to write a tighter and more persuasive letter.

As you revise your draft, imagine how your reader might respond to what you've written. Try to sharpen and condense the message. Before you send off the recommendation, proofread it carefully to ensure that you've left no typos or other errors that might undermine your credibility.

Below is a sample letter, annotated to highlight key components.

To the Hiring Manager:
It is my great pleasure to recommend Susan McCord for employment. I supervised Susan in her job of database manager at Gibbons International for six years.* We are all very sorry that Susan has decided to leave Chicago, but I am very pleased to offer my strongest possible recommendation for her in her new home.†

---

* Rob notes how long he has known Susan, and in what capacity.
† Rob indicates the strength of his support for Susan—his "strongest possible recommendation." The opening paragraph is very strong.

Susan headed a team that provided data for seven diverse groups of our organization, and she always carried out her work with diligence and aplomb. The data division received many requests for data, often sliced into unusual configurations. It's part of marketers' jobs to look for unusual and potentially fruitful patterns in data, and Susan's familiarity with our data and our software made these creative searches very successful. Many requests came in at the last minute, and Susan was ever unflappable, meeting one insane deadline after another.[*]

In spite of her very high-stress and high-stakes position, Susan carried out her responsibilities with an almost superhuman goodwill. She was always a pleasure to be around and happy to do whatever it took to get the job done.

I should also mention that Susan was an exemplary role model and guide for the staff who reported to her. Many of her staff were recent graduates getting their first taste of a "real" job. Susan was brilliant at shepherding these entry-level employees, coaching them through stressful periods, and helping them grow into responsible and productive professionals. Susan's entire team was always ready to accept any challenge with diligence and good humor.[†]

In closing, it is my pleasure to offer Susan my very strongest recommendation.[‡] If I can give you any further information, please do not hesitate to contact me at rstraker@gibbonintl.com.

Sincerely,
Rob Straker

---

[*] Rob supplies a description of Susan's job, the difficulties it entailed, and how Susan successfully coped with those difficulties.

[†] This paragraph gives a vivid sense of what the job was like and describes how Susan made a very special contribution.

[‡] Rob repeats his endorsement of Susan in the closing of the letter.

LinkedIn Recommendations

Recommendations on LinkedIn can provide valuable insights about an individual or a business, and recruiters and hiring managers do look at them. While those recommendations may not make or break an application, they can help. To make the recommendation you write as useful as possible, follow these guidelines:

* Provide a brief summary of how you know the candidate.
* Offer specifics about the candidate's performance, using measurable results wherever possible. Vague comments like "performed well" and "was a pleasure to work with" can do more harm than good, by suggesting that you don't really know the candidate well or even that your recommendation is fake.
* Focus on transferable skills, since you don't know what positions the candidate might be applying for.
* Provide examples of the candidate's performance. Tell a story.
* If you're writing a recommendation for a business owner, focus on how their business stands out from the competition, why you chose to work with them, and how you feel about the outcome.
* Limit the recommendation to 60–100 words.

Thank-yous

Writing a thank-you note appears to be a dying art, particularly in business. The good news is that if you master the art of the thank-you, and practice it regularly, you'll stand out in the crowd of your ungrateful and thoughtless peers.

When should you write a thank-you message in business? There are some circumstances where a thank-you is absolutely required: when someone has written you a recommendation, when you've had a job interview or an informational interview, or when someone's made an introduction that benefited you. There are other situations where a written thank-you is simply gracious: when someone took on some of your work and helped you get across the finish line, when someone gave you some good advice, or when someone helped you overcome an obstacle you couldn't have handled on your own. It's rarely wrong to send a thank-you note, so if you have the impulse, do it.

If you need a reason to send a thank-you beyond simple politeness and gratitude, it's worthwhile to consider that sending a thank-you note can help strengthen your relationship with your reader. A sincere thank-you can leave a lasting impression.

Here are some hints and tips for sending a thank-you message in a business context:

* Keep it appropriate. Your relationship with your reader will help shape the way you write your thank-you. A thank-you to your boss will likely sound different from a thank-you to a peer or someone who reports to you.

* Send your thank-you message promptly.

* Write in your own voice. Sometimes people get nervous when they write thank-you notes, thinking they need to sound more formal or flowery than they usually do. There's no need to dress up your style. Speak from the heart, and write in your usual businesslike manner.

* Be specific about what the action or gesture meant to you. A thank-you for an interview should follow a particular form (see page 171), but a thank-you for help or advice can be more free-flowing. Let your reader know what you're grateful for: how much time and misery they saved you, for example, or how they set you on the right course.

* If appropriate, specifically acknowledge the effort the reader made in your behalf. For instance, if someone spent a lot of time with you or worked through lunch to help you out, be sure to mention it.

For Deeper Connection and Reflection, Write It by Hand

Dominique Schurman

From the very early days of humankind, people have had a deep and profound desire to connect with others through words and symbols. As humans, we have discovered that spoken words, often in one ear and out the other, are not always as lasting or impactful as the written word.

We have seen throughout time that the power and impact of the written word has left lasting legacies in families, in relationships, and in history. From the simple note exchanged between friends, to a personally penned letter from the outgoing president to the new, letters have lasted in our lives, adding value and meaning and, at times, changing the course of our lives.

In this age of e-mail and texts, with phones connected to us twenty-four/seven, is there still room for handwriting in business? I think there is.

First, I believe that the lasting, enduring nature of a penned note, coupled with the personal touch of a handwritten expression, has more meaning than an e-mail or a phone call. Both e-mails and phone calls are fleeting, to be either forgotten or deleted, but the impact, emotion, and essence of a handwritten note or letter will last for days, weeks, months, and years. Frank Blake, the former CEO of Home Depot, spent half a day or more each weekend writing personal notes to company employees. "Our people did amazingly generous things for others," he explained. "It was a great way to end the week." Blake recognized the personal connection forged by the written word. "In an age of email and texts, there is something personal and special about a handwritten note. I have saved every meaningful note I have ever received."[*]

Second, writing by hand can help you reflect in a deep way. In the safe haven of quiet, with only a pen and our thoughts, we sometimes find the courage and the inspiration to reflect in a unique way and, in so doing, perhaps reach a part of ourselves that we otherwise would not have. A recent article in *Harvard Business Review* argues that keeping a journal is an important step in becoming an outstanding leader, and that writing in a physical journal will lead to deeper insights: "writing online doesn't provide the same benefits as writing by hand."[†]

Writing in a journal can offer a means to work through difficult issues and challenging times. The time and space involved in this process enables people to absorb issues, to think them through, and to process them in their own way and in their own time, without the need for an immediate response or reaction. This time to reflect can be tremendously important when stressful matters are at hand.

So even—and, actually, especially—today, in our age of technology and instant everything, the magnitude and importance of the handwritten word plays an ever more important part. Reaching out to another with words on paper may leave a lasting impression that even you may not realize in the moment.

Remember the power of the written word, and write many of

---

[*] Chuck Toney, "Humble at the Top: Why These CEOs Still Write Thank You Notes," *The Chicken Wire* (blog), March 10, 2017, https://thechickenwire.chick-fil-a.com/Lifestyle/Humble-at-the-Top-Why-These-CEOs-Still-Write-Thank-You-Notes.

[†] Nancy J. Adler, "Want to Be an Outstanding Leader? Keep a Journal," *Harvard Business Review*, January 13, 2016, https://hbr.org/2016/01/want-to-be-an-outstanding-leader-keep-a-journal.

them. They will enrich your soul and will inspire those around you in ways that you may never know, leaving a footprint of your life and thoughts.

Dominique Schurman is CEO of Schurman Retail Group, whose brands include Papyrus, Marcel Schurman, Paper Destiny, Niquea.D, Carlton Cards, and Clintons.

Apologies

When you do something regrettable at work, a written apology can go a long way toward making things right. Having the good manners and the courage to say "I'm sorry" shows that you value your relationships at work and that you take responsibility for your actions, and it can create goodwill and strengthen relationships for the future. Apologizing to a customer you've wronged can help you save business you might otherwise have lost.

Before you start writing, though, consider whether a written apology is the best course. Sometimes an in-person apology means more—partly because it takes more courage, partly because meeting face-to-face can strengthen the relationship.

However you choose to apologize, do it as soon as possible after the offending action. Delaying your apology can allow bad feelings to fester and make the situation worse.

YOUR OBJECTIVE

An apology is easier to write if you focus on what you're trying to accomplish. Analyzing your objective might sound silly, but it's easy to stray off message with an apology, especially if you're feeling defensive. Your main purpose is to acknowledge your mistake and tell your reader you're sorry for the distress it caused them. Other possible objectives might be to let your reader know how you're going to fix the problem, if possible, and to assure them that it won't happen again.

CONSIDER YOUR READER

Think a bit about your reader and how he might respond to your apology. What is your relationship? Is your reader your boss, your customer, someone who reports to you? What effect did your action have on him? Is he mad, hurt, insulted? How do you think he'll react to your apology? Considering these questions can help you craft a thoughtful and sincere apology.

SAY YOU'RE SORRY RIGHT UP FRONT

Your message should begin with "I'm sorry." A straightforward expression of regret right at the start lets your reader know you're sincere. Any explanation should come later.

WHAT ELSE DO YOU WANT TO SAY?

It's often helpful for the reader to understand the reason behind your action. Note that a reason is not an excuse. Don't say anything to suggest that what you did was no big deal, and don't try to shift the blame to anyone else, including the reader. An apology that says "I'm sorry, but . . ." doesn't sound sincere. If you're going to apologize, take full responsibility.

You might also let your reader know what you're doing to fix the problem, if that's appropriate, and what you're doing to make sure it never happens again.

Be careful not to say anything in your apology that could create legal liability. If you're apologizing for poor service or a defective product, check with your company's legal department for guidance. If you're apologizing for your own behavior, think about whether legal action over the incident could be possible, and get some advice before you write.

IF SOMETHING FEELS WRONG, FIX IT

Apologies can be tricky, because emotions are often involved. It can be helpful to go through a couple of drafts before you send out your apology. Take a break after you finish your first draft. As you read over it later, think about how your reader might respond. Is the tone sincere? Does the apology really take responsibility for what happened? Will the reader believe that the same kind of thing won't happen again?

Dear Team:

I'm very sorry for missing the deadline yesterday. I know it's put us behind and created more work for Andrea and Cian.

As most of you know, I had deadlines for both TYPE and CCS yesterday. I simply couldn't finish both. I shouldn't have structured my workload that way—I should have known I wouldn't be able to deliver on both.

Again, I'm sorry. I promise to pace my work more sensibly in the future and not to leave you cleaning up my mess.

Best,

Una

PROMOTING YOUR BUSINESS AND YOURSELF

Web Copy

Your company's website is its public face and voice and one of its most powerful tools for sales, marketing, and public relations. Site visitors aren't always aware when they're reading good copy, but they recognize bad copy right away. It's well worth the investment of time and energy to make sure your web copy represents your brand in the best possible way.

NEVER LOSE SIGHT OF YOUR PURPOSE

No matter what kind of business you have, your website is promoting your company, its products and services, its people, and its reputation. Even if you're not explicitly selling on the site, remember that everything on there creates an impression, and put your best foot forward.

UNDERSTAND YOUR READERS

Of course, you won't know exactly who's visiting your website, but it's worthwhile making the effort to understand the types of readers who will be reading your web copy. Who is your target customer or client?

Marketers often create "personas" of their target customers. A persona is a composite portrait of an individual with the characteristics—including sex, age, race, income, education level, family relationships, goals, desires, and other qualities—of the type of person who might be interested in your product or service. Marketers will typically create several personas to represent the target customers of a product or service. When you come up with your own range of personas, give them names.

Once you've constructed a persona, you can use what you know about that individual to write web copy that will appeal to them by addressing their needs, concerns, and interests. What will they be looking for when they visit your site? What will they expect to find? What questions will they have? Your site must address your readers' needs and expectations. As you build the different sections of your site, keep these questions at the front of your mind.

PUT THE IMPORTANT STUFF UP FRONT

The beginnings of web pages are especially important. Research has shown that web users typically read no more than 20 percent of the copy on any given page.*

Take a minute to think about how you interact with web pages.

---

* Jakob Nielsen, "How Little Do Users Read?," Nielsen Norman Group website, May 6, 2008, https://www.nngroup.com/articles/how-little-do-users-read/.

Chances are that when you're shopping for a product or service, you'll visit several sites during your search. If you don't see what you're looking for at the top of a page, you'll probably give up and move on to the next option. So when you're writing copy for your own site, your most important content should go "above the fold"—that is, in the area of the design at the top of the page.

THINK VISUALLY

Think visually when you're writing your web copy, and remember that less is often more. The eye tends to "bounce" off big blocks of text. So to help ensure that your copy will be read, use short sentences, chunk them into short paragraphs, and consider using bullet points to make the content easier to scan. Your copy should accommodate plenty of open space on the page. The copy should work harmoniously with the other graphic elements to create a pleasant user experience.

GET YOUR CONTENT RIGHT

People tend to include too much information on websites, especially people creating sites for small businesses. It's tempting to describe all the features and benefits of your product or service in great detail, but that might be too much for your reader. Your litmus test for content should be "Does it matter to my customer?" That's the content you want to include. Resist the temptation to add more content, even if it's something you're proud of or excited about personally. Don't drown your visitors in excess copy on the page. Every section of your website should be organized around how you can help your customers.

Consider including a call to action on some or all of your pages, encouraging site visitors to contact you or place an order and making it easy for them to do so.

While we're talking about content, we also need to explore how you can use copy to drive visitors to your site. The web is evolving quickly, and you should stay up-to-date on the latest ways search engines locate the terms people search for and direct users to sites. Learn about key words and SEO (search engine optimization). If you're building a site on WordPress or a similar platform, there might be built-in tools you can use to make your site more attractive to searchers; learn about those and take full advantage of them.

ASK TESTERS TO REVIEW YOUR COPY BEFORE YOU FINALIZE IT

In most circumstances, it's pretty easy to change web copy once it's live, so it's not the end of the world if you go live with content that isn't perfect. But web copy is the kind of thing you tend to forget about—and, honestly, you want to be able to forget about it. You want to be confident in the copy you have on your site so you can move on to more important things. So be sure to review the copy once it's on the site, to give yourself a better idea of the experience your users will have.

It's also a good idea to ask a few colleagues or friends to review the site; then you can use their feedback to make improvements. Make sure you let them know specifically what you want feedback on. If you're looking for their reactions to the copy, tell them that. If you vaguely ask them, "What do you think?," you're likely to get random feedback on fonts, colors, images, and so forth. Direct their attention so they can be as helpful as possible.

Blogs

Whether you're running a small business or working for a big one, your business blog can help you maintain contact with current customers and attract new ones. Regular blogging can increase traffic to your web site, and integrating your blog with social media can help you build an online community around your business and your area of expertise.

YOUR PURPOSE IS TO SERVE YOUR AUDIENCE

It's important to pinpoint a purpose for your blog. The risk of not doing so is that your content will be unfocused and you'll end up writing too much that provides too little of value to your readers. Understanding your readers is key to defining your purpose. Here's a useful sentence to fill in as you think about the purpose of your blog: "My blog serves my readers by _____." The answer might be "supplying cutting-edge information about my field" or "providing tools and techniques clients can use." If you keep the focus on serving customers or readers, you're less likely to blather on about topics that are interesting to you but not to your customers.

Having a blog gives you the chance to show off your expertise. Make sure your content is valuable to your readers. People will read your blog as long as they find the content valuable. If they don't, they will move on.

One way to keep readers engaged is to provide variety. It can be hard to find solid subject matter if you're blogging every week. Keep your core focus, but consider writing some posts about complementary topics, for a change of pace. If you're a real estate agent, you can offer tips on renovation or landscaping. If you're a chiropractor, you can discuss nutrition. Consider inviting guest bloggers who are experts in adjacent fields to contribute a blog post now and then (and ask if you can reciprocate, thereby introducing your business and your expertise to their readers).

THE HOOK MATTERS

Think about the last time you read a blog post. Did you read through to the end? Chances are good that you didn't, unless it was a particularly interesting article. Attention spans are short, so you need to ensure that your post starts with an engaging hook that grabs your readers' interest. Once you have your readers' attention, motivate them to read on by front-loading your most important content. Don't save your most critical points for last, or your readers might miss them.

BE CONCISE

Readers sometimes give up on blog posts because there's too much content or there's too much low-quality content. Experts differ on how long the ideal blog post should be, and recommendations about length have changed over time. It's worthwhile doing some research on what works best in terms of length, but it's always a good practice to go through your early drafts and cut out anything that seems superfluous or less engaging than the rest of the content. Your blog post should be long enough to offer useful insights to your readers, but it shouldn't go on longer than it needs to.

MAINTAINING YOUR BLOG

Blog regularly. You don't have to blog every week—that can be a hard pace to maintain—but do pick a regular interval and stick to it. Readers will get discouraged if they come back to your blog and find nothing new.

Share your blog posts on social media. Promoting your blog posts on Twitter, Facebook, and LinkedIn can draw new audiences. You might also want to include a sign-up form on your website so you can e-mail your list, announcing when a new blog post is up.

Consider whether you want to allow comments on your blog. This can be a good way to engage with readers, make connections, and provide even more content to your followers by answering questions. It also means that you'll need to monitor the comments regularly, to get rid of spam posts and moderate any arguments that might flare up. You'll need to assess whether you have the time and if it's worth your energy.

Once you've launched your blog, don't abandon it. A blog with only a few old posts looks dismal. If you find that you can't maintain a regular blog, think about hiding it or archiving the old posts. You can always reactivate the page if you decide to start blogging again.

Social Media

Various forms of social media offer businesses of all sizes the opportunity to connect with customers and potential customers in an entertaining and enriching way. Learning to use social media gives you the chance to provide value to customers between transactions and can help ensure that your customers don't forget you.

Creating Content for Your Website or Blog

Rieva Lesonsky

Content marketing is currently being buzzed about—and for good reason. It's a fast-growing and proven component of marketing plans for small businesses. But since most small business owners didn't major in English or journalism, they can find creating content challenging.

First, it's important to know what makes content effective. Your three top goals should be:

1. Your content needs to be relevant to your market.
2. It should be designed to elicit a response from readers.
3. It should be engaging and interesting.

Next, you need to create a content marketing plan. Components of that plan include:

* Defining your goals. Do you want to get leads? Increase brand awareness? Establish your expertise? Educate your market? Drive traffic to your site or store? Inspire your audience?
* Understanding your audience. What do they want or need to know? To buy? What types of content do they want?
* Picking a voice that will be consistent across your brand. That voice needs to be authentic—and targeted to your potential and current customers and clients.
* Establishing some parameters: How often will you post? What's your budget? Who's responsible for the various tasks?

If your site already has content on it, it's important to review, revise, and update it periodically. Many experts recommend that you add new content to your site at least twice a week. Don't panic; here are some ideas about how you can generate content and still have time to run your business:

* Feature a customer of the week or month. Create a template of five to ten questions and e-mail the list to your customers. Make sure you edit the respondents' grammar before you post their comments.
* Post lists, checklists, or tips. These shouldn't be too long; people don't have time to read through dozens of tips.
* Advertise special offers or promotions.
* Turn your FAQs into blog posts.
* Use guest bloggers.
* Publish product reviews.
* Hire freelancers—if you have the budget.
* Repurpose content: turn blogs into white papers, e-books, podcasts, and videos.
* Run e-mail interviews with relevant people in your industry.
* Educate customers with "how-to" articles.
* Draw on your business's expertise—for example, if you own a food-related business, spotlight recipes.

Two final tips:

1. Use photos, charts, and graphics. Blogs, articles, and social media posts with images get far more views than text-only posts.
2. Don't forget to include a call to action. People need to be told what you want them to do.

And finally, if you're wondering if all this is worth it—the answer is yes. According to TechClient.com, websites with a blog have 434 percent more indexed pages.* That means higher rankings in the search engines.

Rieva Lesonsky is a cofounder and the CEO of GrowBiz Media, a custom content-creation company focusing on small businesses and entrepreneurship, and a co-owner of the blog SmallBizDaily.

* Blogging Statistics—Infographic. http://www.techclient.com/blogging-statistics/.

CHOOSE THE RIGHT PLATFORM(S) FOR YOUR BRAND

There are lots of social media platforms, of course, and each one has a unique personality. Before you take the plunge, do some research to decide which platform or platforms are best for your brand. Consider things like your target demographic and the kind of content you want to share. As I write these words, Twitter has a better reach among young people and African-Americans and Latinos; Facebook has more market penetration with seniors and women. Twitter is better for viral trends, while Facebook is better for building deeper relationships.† But things change fast, and it's important for you to find the most up-to-date information. Not every business needs to be on every platform, and you should make your social media decisions based on the latest information. There will be more entrants to the social media space as time goes by, and some will probably die off, but as long as you do your research, you'll be able to target your activity appropriately.

YOUR PURPOSE IS TO SERVE YOUR CUSTOMERS

Regardless of the platforms you participate in, your objective in using social media is to provide value for your customers and potential customers.

† Lahle Wolfe, "Twitter vs. Facebook: Which Is Better?," The Balance Careers, https://www.thebalance.com/twitter-vs-facebook-which-is-better-3515069.

How can you serve them? What will keep them informed, entertained, and engaged? Concentrate on providing value for them rather than just selling to them. If readers see nothing but selling in your posts, they'll stop following you fast. Focus on what you can give them rather than what you can sell them.

Be careful to keep the content of your social media posts relevant to your business. Posting about personal concerns or politics can alienate customers. An exception is posting about political issues that are directly connected to your business—for example, if you're an accountant, it makes sense to share information about proposed changes to the tax code. Be careful, though, about asking your customers to sign petitions, write letters, and so on. Some might not appreciate being asked to advocate for a political position.

COMMIT TO IT

Launching and maintaining a successful social media presence requires a commitment. It goes without saying that there's a lot of competition online. Nothing looks worse for a business than a halfhearted effort at social media engagement or an abandoned social media account. If you're going to do it, you'll need a strategy that identifies your objectives for social media, and you'll need someone to do the work consistently. Post frequently. You can't disappear.

Obviously, large companies have the resources to have employees dedicated to promoting and maintaining their social media presence. Smaller companies have some more difficult decisions to make. Who is going to post, how often will they post, what kind of content will they post? And what happens when customers or others react? Who handles the ongoing interactions? These are questions you should answer before you launch your social media presence.

FACEBOOK

Facebook is a place where people go to connect with friends and family, and it's a great environment in which to build a community around your organization or brand.

* Keep your updates brief, one to three sentences. People browse Facebook until they find things they want to explore more deeply. They don't want to read a lot of text. Share photos and other images. Text-only updates have much lower engagement than updates with images.

* Use a conversational, friendly tone. In keeping with Facebook's community spirit, your updates should be warm and conversational.

* Use a consistent voice across all your status updates, and express your brand personality.

* Post questions that encourage people to interact. Ask people what they think; ask them to share stories.

* Offer content that's really useful to your customers, and do it frequently. For example, a gardening page could post seasonal tips. An accountant could offer general tax tips. A financial services firm could highlight information about preventing identity theft. If you do this regularly, readers will think of your Facebook page as a useful source of information.

* Share updates from other businesses that provide goods or services that might be interesting to your customers.

* Follow up on readers' comments on your updates. Answer questions that people ask and respond to comments. You're the voice of this community, so engage.

* Learn about Facebook's metrics and keep up with policy changes. Facebook, like all social media outlets, is evolving. Educate yourself about the metrics Facebook uses to determine how much visibility status updates get, and keep up with any changes in these algorithms. A quick Google search can help you become better informed and ensure that more people see your posts.

TWITTER

Twitter is fast-paced and trend-driven. Tweets are typically short—and they fly by fast. Think of tweets like headlines: the point is to convey information quickly and, possibly, to motivate the reader to click on a link.

* Read a lot of tweets. If you're just beginning to tweet for your business, it can take a while to get the hang of writing an effective tweet. Read other companies' tweets. Pay attention to their styles, and develop a distinctive voice for your own brand.
* Tweet regularly. Tweeting only sporadically makes it hard to develop a presence and attract followers.
* Share content that's useful to your customers and potential customers. Retweet interesting content from other businesses. Think about what might interest your followers, and be creative.
* Learn to use hashtags to make your content searchable. Check Twitter's support center for more information about using hashtags effectively.
* Respond to replies, and thank people for retweets. Twitter is all about active engagement.

LINKEDIN

LinkedIn is the platform for business leadership. Individuals use LinkedIn extensively for networking and job seeking, but organizations can also use LinkedIn to connect with potential customers and expand their influence.

* Think about your goals for LinkedIn as you begin to develop your presence there. There's a lot going on, and it's easy to get distracted. Are you looking for new customers, promoting a product, seeking partners, searching for employees? Keep your goal in mind as you craft your LinkedIn presence.
* LinkedIn has extensive support to help you achieve your goals, so explore the LinkedIn Help pages to be sure you're making the most of the platform.

* Create a company page on LinkedIn. It's free, and you can customize it with your logo and a cover image.
* Craft your company description carefully. You have limited space in the template, so focus on what's really important to your customers and clients.
* A complete company profile includes bios of company leaders, career pages where you advertise job openings and share information about company culture, and testimonials from your employees. LinkedIn offers useful articles to help you target these pages more effectively for your customer base.
* As with all forms of social media, you must commit to using LinkedIn and assign someone to keep your LinkedIn presence current with regular updates. These can be company news, or you can share thought leadership articles from other sources, or you can have someone blog on LinkedIn.
* Find followers. A good place to start is with your own people. Ask all your employees to add your company to their personal profiles, and request that they engage with your content by sharing and commenting so that others will see it.
* Consider using sponsored content to extend your reach. Sponsored content allows you to pay to promote company updates to targeted audiences on LinkedIn.

Press Releases

Is your business launching a new product, service, or initiative? Branching out into a new area of business? Have you made an important new hire? You'll want to write a press release to announce the news to the media.

WHAT (AND WHO) A PRESS RELEASE IS FOR

The purpose of a press release is to attract media coverage about news that's important to your organization. Press releases are written to provide content for professional journalists, with the hope that they will choose to write a story about the news.

If you're able to send your press release to a specific journalist, rather than just news organizations, you'll have better luck placing your story. Try to find names of journalists who might be interested in your story.

THINK LIKE A JOURNALIST

Your readers are professional journalists, so you'll need to think like a journalist to make your press release attractive to them. The easier you make it for your readers, the better your chances that they will pick up your news and help disseminate it into the world.

If your press release is successful, journalists may use it as a kind of first draft of their own stories. If you've ever seen multiple articles about the same thing that were written with much of the same language, it's because those writers were all working from the same press release and relying on it as basis for their own stories. Sometimes journalists will even use the press release as the story, making very few changes. For this reason, you need to think like a journalist when you write your press release, and style it like a news story. Write the article you'd like to see in the news, with complete information. You can make it easier for journalists to pick up the story if you provide them with clean, clear copy, with short sentences and simple vocabulary. Unless you're targeting the press for a specific industry, try to avoid technical jargon. If you must use technical vocabulary, be sure to provide straightforward definitions that the average reader can understand.

START STRONG

Part of writing like a journalist is constructing a strong opening, with your most important information in your first paragraph. Imagine that your readers will read only the first paragraph of the press release and no more—make sure they can get the main points of the story. Your first paragraph should answer the journalist's questions: *who, what, when, where, why,* and *how.*

Writing like a journalist also means using an "inverted pyramid" structure: the broadest, most general information goes at the beginning of the press release, and the information becomes more specific and detailed as you go along. Put the most important information at the beginning, so that if readers stop reading they will not have missed anything critical.

MAKE SURE YOUR NEWS IS NEWSWORTHY (AND WRITE IT AS NEWS)

Why should anyone care about your news? If you work for a large organization, things like high-level hires, new products, and market entries will be of interest to the business press. If you run a small business, it can be more challenging to show that your business is newsworthy. As you plan your press release, think from the point of view of the end reader—someone in the community who would like to know about your new day-care business, accounting firm, or yoga studio, for example. What's newsworthy or remarkable about it? Even if your business is just filling a gap in the community, it might be considered newsworthy.

You may be hoping that the press release will attract attention to your business, but your press release should be written as news, not as promotional copy. Focus on the facts, on telling the story. Don't slip into selling, and don't use emotional language or make claims that are not factual.

USE THE STANDARD FORMAT

A press release should follow a traditional, standard format. If you want journalists to take you seriously, make sure your press release appears in this format:

FOR IMMEDIATE RELEASE (or specify the release date)
Contact person and full contact information
Headline
City, state (or country), date

First paragraph: present the essence of the message, including
the answers to who, what, when, where, why, and how?

Middle paragraphs: these should be brief and easy to scan.

Bottom of page 1 (if the press release continues onto a second
page): type -more- (the word "more" flanked by hyphens).

Top of the next page: abbreviated headline

Page 2: the remainder of the text

Restate your contact information after the last paragraph.

End of the press release: use the symbol # # # to indicate that
the press release is finished.

FIX IT BEFORE YOU SEND IT

You're wise to go through several drafts of a press release, especially if
you are not experienced in writing them. Your first drafts will likely
be too long and unfocused. As you revise, make sure you're providing
only the most essential information about the news item. Limit yourself to two pages: the longer you go on, the less of your readers' attention you'll have, so be sure your press release is tight and engaging. And
always provide your contact information, so that readers can reach you
if they want to receive additional information.

For sample press releases and a template you can use, visit me at
www.howtowriteanything.com.

Speeches

By some accounts, roughly 25 percent of Americans fear public speaking. Luckily, good preparation can build your confidence and help
make your speech a great experience for yourself and your audience.
You can relieve a lot of the worry about giving a speech by taking an
analytical approach to it.

LET YOUR PURPOSE GUIDE YOU

What's the purpose for your speech? Do you want to inspire, educate,
persuade, entertain, or some combination of these? Have the event

organizers given you any guidance about what they want from your speech? Decide on an objective for your speech, and let that objective guide the way you develop it. If you get sidetracked as you write your speech, come back and ask yourself, "What's my objective?"

UNDERSTAND WHAT YOUR AUDIENCE NEEDS AND EXPECTS

Your audience for a speech is, obviously, composed of listeners rather than readers. That knowledge will guide the way you write your speech, but it won't change the way you analyze your audience. How much do you know about them? You should feel free to consult the organizer if you're not sure who you'll be speaking to. What do they think and believe? What will they expect from you? What topic would most engage them? Try putting yourself in the shoes of your audience members and imagine listening to the speech you have planned. How can you best serve their needs?

It can help to imagine a model listener, a specific person in the audience. Who is she? What does she know about the topic? What does she care about? What can you share with her that will interest her? Imagining a single listener can be easier than writing a speech for a crowd.

START STRONG AND SPECIFIC

A speech needs a strong opening to grab the attention of the audience. Starting with a joke is a time-honored tradition. Not everyone thinks it's a good idea. If you do decide to start with a joke, make sure it's one that this particular audience will enjoy.

A joke works because it's a kind of icebreaker. Other, more substantive, types of openings include anecdotes, quotations, and problem statements. The rest of your speech should follow naturally from your opening—showing how the anecdote is relevant, expanding on the message of the quotation, or exploring how to solve the problem. Your objective is to hook your audience and make them interested in listening to your speech.

CONTENT

It goes without saying that the topic of your speech should be something that will appeal to your listeners. If you have doubts, consider contacting the event organizer with a few different possible topics and asking for her opinion on which one would be best. Everyone involved in the event wants your speech to succeed, so you can count on getting good advice from the organizer.

Once you've selected a topic, you need to decide on the scope. Remember that people will be listening rather than reading, so limiting the scope of your treatment and keeping your approach fairly simple is a good idea. Don't feel you need to give a complete or comprehensive treatment of the topic. Rather than present an exhaustive account of something, choose a particularly interesting angle and explore it. Plan to talk about no more than three main points in your speech. In general, you can demand more in the way of attention from readers than you can from listeners.

You're wise to write out your entire speech, even if you think you might be inclined to go off-script a little bit during the delivery. Writing it all out will force you to decide exactly what you want to say, in what degree of depth. It's also a great way of calming your nerves. Standing up and winging it can be unnerving, especially if you're not used to it, so having the whole text in front of you can boost your confidence. (Make sure you print it out or display it on your tablet in a larger font than normal; you don't want to be squinting to make out what you've written.)

As you draft, keep in mind that the average speech proceeds at about 120 words per minute. Use this to gauge length. Expect to go through several drafts. It's wise to ask a colleague or friend to read a draft of your speech or—even better—to listen to you practice and give you feedback on your presentation. As you rehearse, you'll find areas you want to revise—for instance, language that looks fine on the page but doesn't sound right spoken aloud or is difficult to articulate. You might find that the rhythm doesn't feel right and that you want to vary the length of your sentences. You might also find missing content, or that your

The Art of the Anecdote

Rachel Christmas Derrick

I had been nodding off in my high school library when I finally turned to the book we had just been assigned on the Chinese Revolution of 1949. Annoyed at the length of this big fat volume, I reluctantly began to read. Suddenly, I was watching a woman gather her two children and whatever belongings she could snatch up as she raced from her home, pulling her stumbling toddlers with her, knowing she could never return. I was hearing the battling thoughts of a man as he alternated between hope for a better life and the terror of the unknown.

This thick book turned out to be one of the most captivating and memorable I ever read. By putting faces on specific events during that tumultuous historic period, the author enabled me to digest and more easily remember the extremely complex sociopolitical issues of the time.

Even in business writing, storytelling can mean the difference between engaging a reader and inducing yawns. The art of the anecdote—a brief, humanizing tale to illustrate or underscore a point—is worth mastering.

No matter what business you're in, the ultimate goal is to have some kind of impact on human beings. First, consider your endgame: (1) Who is your audience? and (2) What, exactly, do you want them to do, think, or feel as a result of reading what you write? Then find a human-focused story (perhaps to start your piece with) that steers readers toward your objective by bringing your main point to life.

And by "human-focused," I don't mean that your anecdote has to be about people, necessarily. But whether it's a tale of a dog that eats only your company's gourmet treats or a derelict house that was finally renovated thanks to your firm's investment advice, the story will be most powerful if it shows (instead of *telling* readers about) an impact on human lives, either direct or indirect.

Can't think of a good real-life example? Poetic license allows you to make one up—drawing on legitimate experiences, of course. For instance, when I started reading that book on the Chinese Revolution, I was actually at home, not in my high school library. I was able to get to my point faster, however, by using fewer words; "high school library" worked more efficiently than saying that I was at my desk at home, then explaining that I was a high school student at the time. As long as you don't claim it actually happened, you can even use a composite experience, such as a story about a woman in Nebraska who "looks out her window and sees . . ." instead of writing, "My neighbor looked out her window and saw. . . ." Bottom line: think of an anecdote that will engage your particular audience right away. Your readers will then be open to the rest of what you want to tell them.

Rachel Christmas Derrick is a freelance writer and the director of communication and fund-raising at the Urban Homesteading Assistance Board, an affordable-housing nonprofit.

speech is too long. Don't wait till the last minute to start this process of practicing and polishing—give yourself plenty of time.

As you write, clearly mark the transitions for your listeners. If a reader loses the train of your argument, he can go back and reread; a listener doesn't have this luxury. Offer brief summaries as you go along, and clearly state when you're shifting perspectives. If you're talking about events in the past, make sure your listeners will understand where they are on your timeline. Let your readers know when you're wrapping things up. It can be very jarring to hear a speech that ends in a way that feels abrupt. A little "hand-holding" for your listeners throughout the speech can improve their experience markedly.

Speaking of conclusions: put some extra effort into finishing with a punch. Provide a conclusion that the audience will remember—sum up your points, end with a compelling story, or do something else to tie a nice bow on your speech. Leave the audience nodding in agreement or smiling.

Finally, make sure that the length of the final (and rehearsed) speech falls within the time guidelines you've been given. Don't exceed your time limit—plan to come in slightly under it. Don't cheat and try to sneak in a few more points. You're better off leaving your audience wishing for more, not wishing you'd go away.

Bios

A business bio tells, briefly, the story of your career. It's not meant to be comprehensive. Rather, it highlights the most important events of your career and explains a bit about how you got where you are and what value you offer. Bios are used for different purposes—on company websites and pitch documents, to introduce you as a speaker or presenter, and for other business-related events.

If you're having trouble getting started, consider if there's someone you can ask for a few samples to use as models. Bios on company websites often follow a standard format. LinkedIn is also a good source of bios you can use for inspiration.

CONSIDER YOUR PURPOSE

The objective of a bio is to tell your story, not to provide an exhaustive account of all your activities. Depending on the purpose of the bio, the story you tell might be one of the following:

* "I have a lot of experience doing the kind of thing you need done. You can feel confident about recruiting or hiring me."

* "I'm an expert on this topic; you'll enjoy hearing what I have to say or getting my advice."
* "My accomplishments are impressive. I'll be an asset to any company that hires or retains me."

Many businesspeople keep several different versions of their bio available, tailored for different uses.

GET YOUR CONTENT RIGHT

The purpose of the bio will guide the content you include. Think about who will be reading the bio, what they might be expecting to see, and what will make an impression on them. Bios for company websites and pitch decks should highlight your experience solving the kinds of problems your customers want solved. Bios for speaking engagements and charity events can range more widely and can include your philanthropic activities. Your profile summary on LinkedIn should be personally engaging and position you for your next role. You should mention key positions at companies where you've worked. You can also highlight particular projects you've worked on and the results you've achieved on those projects.

Think about the arc of your career as you brainstorm for your bio. What were the major turning points in your career? What values and interests drove some of the decisions you made? How do all the parts add up to the current whole? Remember that a bio is not a résumé in prose format. It's a synthesis of the experiences and achievements that make you unique.

Don't rely on impressive-sounding client lists to take the place of an in-depth bio. Remember, your bio is meant to tell your story, so use the opportunity not just to list facts and figures but also to show what makes you a particularly valuable individual.

Honor any obligations to confidentiality you may have as you write your bio. You might not be at liberty to talk about certain deals or particular customers or clients. However, you might be able to discuss the experience if you keep the focus on your role and your achievements.

It's conventional to write your bio in the third person, as though you were writing about someone else. Use an objective tone, and stick to the facts. Some bios can be written in the first person—for example, for an entrepreneur's website or for a LinkedIn profile summary.

POLISH BEFORE YOU FINALIZE

Your first draft will probably be too long. It can take a few drafts for you to streamline the story of your career. Keep your bio brief—one page or less. The more senior you become, the more challenging it will be to restrict yourself to this length. Always ask yourself what's really important about the arc of your career and the development of your interests, and avoid getting bogged down in details.

KEEP IT UPDATED

The world changes fast, and your bio should keep up. It's a good idea to have an updated bio and résumé on hand in case an opportunity pops up unexpectedly. Whenever you change jobs, get a promotion, or achieve a notable goal at work, you should update your résumé, bio, and LinkedIn profile.

SAMPLE BIO

Below is a sample bio, the sort a businessperson might post on the company website.

Maxwell Senna leads Selpat's Rotary Division in China and has a deep passion for serving clients in the industrial sectors in Asia and Australia.

He has worked with some of Asia's leading manufacturers in operational transformations and has been an adviser to many governmental commissions on manufacturing efficiency and standards. Outside his client work, Maxwell is a founder of Forum for Innovation, a platform that combines business, academia, and government to drive dialogue and develop concrete proposals for sustainable and eco-friendly manufacturing processes. He also serves on the board of ETICA, a nonprofit that encourages girls to explore careers in engineering, and on the board of one of Shanghai's leading independent schools.

Maxwell joined Selpat in 2004. Prior to joining Selpat, he worked at DBH Industries as a senior engineer in South America and China.

EMPLOYMENT MATTERS

Résumés

Your résumé is more than just a record of your employment history. Through careful selection and presentation of information, a résumé should tell a story and present you as a great fit for the position you're applying for. You should be prepared to revise your résumé for each position you apply to; sometimes small adjustments can make a big difference in whether or not companies decide to interview you.

WHAT'S YOUR OBJECTIVE?

What's your objective when you write a résumé? Obviously, you're looking for a job, but no one gets a job offer from a résumé alone. The résumé is but one step on the path to employment. In conjunction with your cover letter, your résumé should lead the reader to a conclusion— that conclusion being "I want to interview this person."

So your objective is an interview, not a job. It might seem like a subtle distinction, but it's an important one. As you work on your résumé, keep this question in the front of your mind: "How can I interest them enough to want to interview me?"

WRITE FOR YOUR READER

You don't know the individual who will be reviewing your résumé, of course, but if you have a job description, you know a lot about what that person is looking for. Pay close attention to the job description, compare it closely with your résumé, and make sure your résumé matches up as nearly as possible (while remaining scrupulously honest about your experience and qualifications).

In some cases, your first "reader" will be scanning software rather than a human being. To get over this first hurdle, be sure your résumé includes the keywords listed in the job description. It's even better if the keywords appear more than once. Just dropping keywords into the "Skills" section of the résumé won't cut it; robots are smarter than that. You need to make the effort to integrate the keywords into the résumé.

This integration is important. If you make it through this first screening, your résumé will be read by a human with a critical eye, so you must ensure that your résumé makes a compelling case that you're a good fit for the position.

Beginnings Count

You have less than ten seconds to grab the attention of the person reading your résumé, so what you put at the beginning counts. You should make the most of that space at the top of the résumé, and motivate the reader to spend time looking further.

Experts disagree about whether you should begin your résumé with an objective, but most argue that objectives are old-fashioned. Unless they're well executed and do more than state the obvious ("I'm seeking a job"), they actually delay the reader from reaching the core information on the résumé. There's one exception to this rule, though, and that's when you're making a big jump in career field. If all your work experience is in Field A and you're applying for a job in Field B, the reader is going to be confused by your résumé unless you include an objective explaining, briefly, that you are making the change and why you think your background makes you a good candidate for a job in this new field.

For everyone else, the objective section of the résumé has been replaced with a résumé summary statement. A summary statement usually consists of three to five bullet points that describe what's unique about you. They don't just recap information from the résumé—they synthesize your experience into a coherent whole. They sum up your strengths, your skills, and how you can add value to the company or the team you would be on.

As you work on your summary statement, think from the point of view of your reader—in this case, the hiring manager. If you were hiring for this position, what kind of person would you hope to find? What kind of qualities and experience would the ideal candidate have? Keeping the answers to these questions in mind can help you as you weed through your own experience and decide what to include in your summary.

Whether you begin your résumé with an objective or a summary statement, you should plan to revise this beginning as needed for each job you apply for. It's a lot of work, but sending nontargeted, generic résumés off into the blue is not a good way to find a job. If you're going to spend the time sending out résumés, it's worthwhile to invest a little extra time to tailor them to the individual jobs you're applying for.

Get Your Content Right

Depending on how much work experience you have and what your career history looks like, you might have quite a lot of leeway in terms of what content you choose for your résumé. You don't have to be comprehensive; you don't have to note every job you've ever had.

Gaps in employment are still a red flag for most employers. If you have a significant gap on your résumé, you should plan to explain it in the cover letter you include in your job application.

Be Concise

Unless you are a senior employee or have extensive experience that's relevant to the job you're applying for, you're wise to keep your résumé to one page. It can be challenging to condense your experience into one page, but it's a good challenge. Keeping the résumé to one page will force you to choose the most relevant and persuasive information to include.

If you are more senior, your résumé will probably need to extend beyond one page, but it should still be a selective representation of your experience, not a detailed and complete accounting of everything you've ever done.

Be Sure It's Perfect Before You Send It

Typically, someone with a pile of résumés in front of him is looking harder for a reason to say no than a reason to say yes. Be sure your résumé is as perfect as it can be before you send it out, and don't let carelessness give the reader an excuse to put it in the "no" pile without reviewing your qualifications carefully.

Working on a résumé can be tedious, and almost everyone reaches the point where they want to send it out and never look at it again. Resist this temptation. Proofread your résumé carefully. Recruit one or two eagle-eyed friends to proofread it for you. Sending out a résumé with typos or other errors can give prospective employers the idea that you're careless or not that interested in the job.

Before you send it off, take the time to review the résumé against the job description one more time, and ensure that you're making the best possible case that you're a good fit for the job.

Taking those few extra minutes to polish and perfect your résumé can mean the difference between rejection and an invitation to interview.

Cover Letter for Your Résumé

Your cover letter is an important part of your job application; don't neglect it. There's no sense in working painstakingly on your résumé if you're going to slap a careless cover letter on top of it. Take the time to craft your cover letter carefully, and be sure you revise it for each job you apply for. Your cover letter should reflect the research you've done about the organization and your understanding of the position.

Get the Ask Clear

Your purpose in writing a cover letter is *not* to ask for a job—it's to ask for an interview. Understanding this distinction should make it easier to craft your letter. Your objective is to make a case to the hiring manager that she should bring you in for an interview.

Write for Your Reader

Your cover letter is your chance to address the hiring manager (or whoever is screening the résumés) directly as a human being. Make the most of it.

Put yourself in your reader's shoes as you craft your cover letter. What are her needs and expectations? What kind of candidate is she hoping to meet? What information will make her put your résumé into the "maybe" file rather than the much larger "no" file?

Make the salutation of your letter as specific as you can. If you have the name of an individual, use it. Even "To the hiring manager" is a better salutation than "To whom it may concern."

Start Strong and Specific

The first paragraph of your cover letter is important. State the position you're applying for (the company might be running multiple searches). If you're writing at the suggestion of a mutual acquaintance, say so and mention how you know that person. Express your interest in the position, and say briefly why you're interested. Wrap up your first paragraph by briefly explaining why you think you're a great fit for the job.

Be Concise

The challenge of a cover letter is to make a strong case that you're a good fit, and to do so on one page. More senior hires can submit longer letters, but be considerate of your reader's time, and be sure that whatever you write is directly relevant to the position you're applying for.

Get the Content Right

Tailor your cover letter to the particular job you're applying for. It helps to develop a few different templates to use as the basis for your different letters, but be sure the cover letter you send is customized to the job you're applying for.

Draw your reader's attention to information on the résumé that is particularly relevant to your application for this particular job. Don't just restate the information on the résumé; elaborate on it. This is your chance to argue your case; use your letter to make explicit what's implicit in the résumé itself.

Your focus should be on what you have to offer the employer, not what the job can offer you. It's great to say you're excited about the job and that you think you would enjoy it, but remember to think from your reader's point of view and expand on how you can meet their needs.

It can be helpful to demonstrate some knowledge of the organization in your cover letter, but don't go overboard. Mention the company's history or reputation only if you can link it to something specific in your background or your interests—for example, if the company is working on an initiative that you could contribute to. Simply saying that it would be great to work for Google, for instance, doesn't advance your case.

FIX IT BEFORE YOU SEND IT

Typos, spelling mistakes, and other errors can throw you out of the running immediately, so ensure that your letter is *perfect* before you submit it. Be sure your tone is professional. This is not the time for humor or informal language. You must show that you're able to communicate in a formal, professional manner.

For sample cover letters, visit me at www.howtowriteanything .com.

Follow-up Message After a Job Interview

The follow-up message you send after a job interview is a special kind of thank-you note. It goes beyond a simple statement of thanks and can be an important part of your overall application and interview process. Be sure to send your follow-up soon after the interview. A prompt thank-you can help you stand out from the crowd.

BE STRATEGIC ABOUT YOUR PURPOSE

With a post-interview follow-up, you're not only thanking the interviewer for his time, you're also reaffirming your interest in the position and expanding on what happened during the interview. Really think about the conversation during the interview and how your message can deepen it.

WRITE FOR YOUR READER

It's natural to be very focused on yourself during the job interview process, so make the effort now to consider your reader and his position. Don't write a vague, pro forma note; use this opportunity to connect with the reader and extend the conversation you had during the interview.

In your closing, wish the reader luck in finding the best candidate for the position. Of course you're hoping that this candidate will be you, but it's professional and gracious to acknowledge that it might not be.

GET YOUR CONTENT RIGHT

Open your follow-up message with a statement of thanks to the interviewer, and let her know you enjoyed meeting her. Reaffirm your interest in the position. If something that happened during the interview increased your interest in the job, say so, and say why. Don't focus only on what the job might do for you; expand on the contribution you could make in the organization.

Be sure to include something specific from the interview; if you have additional thoughts to share about a topic you discussed, you can mention them briefly.

The trick here is keeping it brief and to the point. You want to show that you were engaged in the interview and have given the discussion further productive thought, but you don't want to write pages and pages of follow-up. Limit this section to a few sentences. Avoid speculating about what you might do in the job and changes you would make if you are hired.

If you have experience or qualifications that you did not have a chance to discuss during the interview, you can mention them in your follow-up. You should also offer to provide any additional information about yourself the company might require, and indicate that you are available for another meeting. Don't be too pushy at this point, and don't assume that you'll get a second interview. Indicate your interest, and leave it at that.

FIX IT BEFORE YOU SEND IT

Your follow-up message is every bit as important as your initial cover letter, so you should take extra care to make sure it's perfect before you send it out. Proofread it carefully. Ask a friend or family member to review it for errors. Don't run out of energy at this point. You could be very close to getting a job offer. Make sure your follow-up letter reflects well on you rather than looking like a slapdash effort.

Five Tips for Communicating with Millennials in the Workplace

Sydney Strauss

It's a cliché because it's true: each generation has something unique and valuable to bring to the table. It is a shame that so much of this potential energy can get lost in translation across generations, and perhaps the worst part is that it's totally avoidable. To ensure the utmost success in the workplace, we should really all start making it a priority to practice cross-generational communication. After all, when we can understand each other, we can work together; and when we can work together, we can succeed together.

As a millennial myself, I know that our style of communication can seem especially idiosyncratic to a lot of people. If you're discouraged by that seemingly massive barrier, don't worry; getting through to us is a lot simpler than you might think. I promise that we millennials have a lot to offer, and that your efforts will prove to be worthwhile for everybody.

1. **Empathize.** Keep in mind that, for us, *the workplace can often be an anxious space.* We feel sure that baby boomers don't like us, and our economic post–Great Recession anxiety is through the roof. You might perceive millennials as timid or uninterested, but the truth is that we're just anxious; we have a million and one opinions, but we're just not sure anyone wants to hear them. Let this knowledge inform all your communications with millennials.

2. **Encourage openness.** You stand to gain a whole lot when your millennial colleagues are sharing their insights with the whole team. Again, each generation has a unique and useful perspective; hearing the millennial angle in particular could help your company reach a younger demographic, improve on social media marketing, or find the right cause or charity to get involved with, for example. A lot of millennials are brand-new to the workforce, so they might be unfamiliar with the dynamics of team meetings—a simple "What do you think?" in their first meeting or two could really expedite their acclimation process.

3. **Embrace new technology.** It's no secret that millennials are natives when it comes to modern technology, and it shows in our preferred methods of communication (texting instead of phone calls, for example). Adapting to some of these modern platforms is not only a surefire way to get a prompt response from a millennial but can

also be a crucial step forward for your company in the face of an ever-changing business world.

4. **Discuss the big picture.** Generally speaking, millennials are eager for their work to be a part of something impactful; they will be at the top of their game as employees if they know that they're working toward something bigger than themselves. Putting a big goal like "going green" at the forefront of discussions will not only keep your millennial employees enthusiastic but will also promote growth and long-term goal setting for the future of the company.

5. **Be transparent.** You may have heard that we need to be let down easy, but the truth is that we thrive on constructive criticism and prefer to hear things without the sugarcoating. We are very eager for our own growth as professional people, so the less time wasted the better—this is easier for everyone involved. We will be able to make improvements much more quickly if you are honest and transparent with your feedback. No hard feelings.

Sydney Strauss is a writer based in the Pacific Northwest.

Job Descriptions

In most large organizations, writing job descriptions is a collaboration between HR and the department and manager who will be working with the new hire. Many companies have templates you can use as a jumping-off point. In smaller companies, managers are often on their own creating job descriptions. Whatever the size of your organization, it will be worth your time to craft your job descriptions carefully.

BE SURE YOU KNOW WHAT YOU'RE LOOKING FOR

As you start writing your job description, be sure you know what the job actually entails. Of course, many positions evolve over time, and it can be especially difficult to pin down a brand-new role. But making the effort to define the role and writing an accurate description of it can save you, your colleagues, and job applicants a great deal of time and trouble—and it can also help ensure that you hire the right person.

A job description outlines the functions and requirements of the job and describes where the role sits within the organization. It may also provide a framework for conducting a performance review, which makes it all the more important to get it right before you start interviewing.

GET THE CONTENT RIGHT

An accurate and complete job description should contain the following information:

Basic information: job title, department, supervisor (including dotted-line supervisor relationships), and salary range.

Job functions: a list of the duties to be performed and the objectives related to those duties. Duties are usually listed in order of importance and are sometimes broken out into percentages. (Don't include nonessential duties that make up less than 5 percent of the job.)

Requirements: candidate requirements are listed in order of importance. This section is sometimes divided into "Minimum Requirements" and "Preferred Requirements." (Consider carefully how you designate requirements; you can scare away qualified applicants if you define too many minimum requirements.)

Special Requirements: these might include required testing, licenses, clearances, and the like.

Some companies include an "Ideal Candidate" section to describe the exact set of qualifications, background, and attitude they are seeking in a candidate. Whether or not you decide to include one in the final job description, the process of developing an "Ideal Candidate" section can help you refine exactly what you want for the position.

Including a section about your organization's culture, values, and mission can also be helpful. This information allows potential applicants to decide for themselves if they might be a good fit, and it can also help them prepare for an interview.

Dealing with salaries in job descriptions can be tricky. Some organizations state "salary commensurate with experience." This kind of vague statement, though, can deter people from applying and can elicit applications from unqualified or underqualified candidates. Most companies have a policy about how to list salary requirements in job descriptions. If you're running your own small company, it might be wise to list a salary range.

GET IT RIGHT BEFORE YOU RELEASE IT INTO THE WORLD

Don't post an out-of-date or inaccurate job description, figuring you will fix it later or redefine the job during interviews. Especially if you're creating a new role or significantly revising an existing one, it's worthwhile going through several drafts and asking colleagues to review them, especially the managers or supervisors who will work with the new hire. Ensure that the job description you release into the world is as accurate as you can make it.

Job Advertisements

A good job advertisement can attract great candidates; a poor one can attract crowds of applicants who don't quite fit. It's worth making the effort to craft a job ad that describes the job and the company accurately and that inspires the right kind of candidates to apply.

START STRONG

Job seekers are plowing through lots of job descriptions. You want yours to stand out and to excite the right kind of applicant. To that end, your first step should be understanding exactly the kind of applicant you would like to hire. Who is your ideal candidate? Make two lists: the key requirements for the job and the characteristics of your ideal hire. If you're not the person who will be supervising the new hire, talk to the person who will be and learn what their hopes are for the position. Then spend some time jotting down notes about the company or organization. What is the culture like? What are the people like? What is the organization trying to achieve, and what's it like to work there?

Use Templates to Speed Your Work

If there's a particular type of document you write frequently, you should consider developing a template for it so you don't have to start from scratch every time. Documents like job descriptions lend themselves naturally to this process, but anything you write frequently probably has an underlying structure that you can distill into a template. One of my clients worked for an executive search firm and frequently wrote letters describing candidates to potential employers. We developed a candidate letter template, with an introductory paragraph, a second paragraph about the candidate's background, a third paragraph about the fit between the candidate and the job, and a fourth paragraph about the candidate's level of interest in the position. My client was then able to speed his writing by using the framework, which was flexible enough to be customized for special circumstances.

Do you find yourself writing the same sort of thing over and over again? If so, it's probably worth the investment of time now to craft a template that will save you time in the future.

GET THE CONTENT RIGHT

If you're posting on a site like Indeed or Glassdoor, take advantage of any templates or guidance the site offers. Look at listings for similar jobs and use them as models. Your job description should contain a brief account of the organization and its mission as well as a sketch of the work environment. Provide a detailed, bulleted list of the requirements of the role. Mention benefits like insurance, vacation time, retirement, and so on. Include other perks, like flex time, telecommuting, and tuition reimbursement. Consider how you want to handle salary—many companies offer a salary range to help ensure that they get appropriate applicants. If your minimum requirements really are the minimum, say so: include a statement specifying that only candidates who meet the stated qualifications will be considered. Include information about how to apply.

FIX IT BEFORE YOU POST IT

Chances are that your first draft will be too long. The ad should not contain the entire job description, only the key requirements. Check your draft for clichés like "self-starter," "team player," and "highly motivated." These are so overused that they don't add value; they just take up space. Be sure you haven't hyped the job so much that you've neglected to provide real substance about the position and the company. If the ad reads like a sales letter or a promotion for a holiday camp, tone it down. Finally, ensure that you've been entirely honest. If the salary offered is below average, don't say your compensation is "competitive." Creating false expectations can lead to unnecessary disappointment and wasted time.

For sample job descriptions, visit me at www.howtowriteanything .com.

Performance Reviews

Writing a performance review can be a challenge for a couple of reasons. First, it's not something you do every day, even if you're an experienced manager. Second, performance reviews can have a lasting impact, so there's pressure to be fair and accurate. Big companies with a lot of employees usually offer supervisors guidelines for writing performance reviews; if you have that resource, be sure to take full advantage of it.

GETTING STARTED

First, it should go without saying that you must maintain confidentiality throughout the process. Allow yourself plenty of time to gather information and write the review. Don't start at the last minute. You might want to consider asking the employee to participate by drafting her own self-evaluation. When employees participate in the process, they feel valued and heard. They're also more likely than you are to understand the nuances of the job and the challenges they've faced during the year. As you reflect, be sure you're considering the full year, not just recent happenings. To jog your memory, review your e-mails.

GET THE CONTENT RIGHT

Make sure your review includes both positives and areas for improvement. Even a problematic employee has had some successes, and even the best employee has room to develop. Handled right, a performance review should recognize achievements and help support employees in their growth over the coming year. Be specific: cite particular projects or activities where the employee has performed well or fallen short. Look forward as well as backward, and propose some goals for the coming year: training programs, new responsibilities, anything you think might help the employee develop. As you write, use neutral, descriptive language. Don't show emotion, and don't make any personal comments.

FIX IT BEFORE YOU FINALIZE

If you can, let a few days pass between your first and final drafts; this will allow you to develop some perspective on what you've written. Be sure you haven't engaged in lavish praise or harsh criticism. Your tone should be moderate and professional. If you've praised an employee as the best you've ever seen in that position, it might be difficult to terminate her later should things change. If you've written a very unkind review, the employee might cite it if he contests a future dismissal. If there have been problems with the employee's performance, be sure you've indicated accurately how serious they are: is the employee at risk of termination, or are there some areas for improvement? Your review should paint an accurate picture of employee performance in a professional way.

For sample performance reviews, visit me at www.howtowriteany thing.com.

WRITING YOUR OWN PERFORMANCE REVIEW

If you've been asked to do a self-assessment as part of your performance review, you have an opportunity to make the experience more positive and take steps toward your growth in the organization. You can help your boss and yourself by putting some effort into your own performance review.

Here are some tips as you prepare your self-evaluation:

* Be sure you understand what areas you're being asked to cover in your self-assessment. If you don't, ask.
* Don't be too modest. Research shows that most employees rate themselves lower than their managers would. Don't hide your light under a bushel. Many people feel embarrassed about praising themselves. If you're struggling with modesty or embarrassment, try to look at yourself from an objective perspective. Imagine you're evaluating the performance of someone who works for you. What has that person done really well? Where could he improve? Sometimes taking a step back can help you evaluate your own strengths and weaknesses more fairly.
* Use the opportunity to shape the discussion about problem areas. If you know your manager is unhappy about something, address the problem in your self-evaluation and present your perspective on it. Consider proposing solutions.

* Be objective and neutral. If you feel that something is being mishandled, don't put your boss on the spot. Find a detached way to raise the issue and suggest alternative approaches.
* Consider asking your colleagues to give you an honest appraisal of your performance as a co-worker.
* Highlight specific achievements and specific areas where you would like to improve. Your boss won't remember the year you had as well as you do, and it will be helpful for you to bring out details to review and discuss.

Resignation Letters

Whatever your reason for leaving your job, it's worthwhile handling your resignation letter professionally and leaving behind a good impression.

The best practice is to tender your resignation in person, then to follow up your conversation with a formal letter of resignation.

How much you say in your resignation letter is up to you. Whether you choose to keep it brief or share more information, be sure to keep it businesslike.

YOUR PURPOSE

At its most basic, the purpose of a resignation letter is to share your intent to resign and let your employer know what your last day of work will be. Depending on the circumstances of your departure, you might also want to foster a sense of goodwill in your letter for the purpose of future relationships.

KEEP IT BRIEF

A resignation letter does not need to be long and detailed. A perfectly acceptable bare-bones letter will state your intention to resign, the date of your resignation, and nothing more.

If you want to expand a bit, it's courteous to offer a reason for your resignation. Keep your language neutral, even if you're leaving because of a bad situation. Don't use the letter to express anger or frustration or to let your boss know what a bad job she's doing. Don't blame others. You're leaving; just say so and move on. Venting about your experience does no good, it can hurt your reputation, and you'll probably regret it later.

If you feel able to do so, say something nice about your experience at the organization. Did you enjoy your colleagues? Did you appreciate the challenge of the job? Did you learn a lot? You never know when goodwill from a former employer might come in handy.

If you're willing to help with the transition to your successor, you can mention that in the letter.

Close your letter by thanking your reader. Your thanks don't have to be effusive, but it's a courteous way to wrap up the letter.

CHECK IT BEFORE YOU SEND IT

Be sure to check your tone before you send in your resignation. It should be businesslike and cordial, not angry or passive-aggressive. If you're angry, it might help to write out everything you're feeling and put that draft aside. Then start fresh and compose a neutral and professional resignation letter. If you're not sure your tone is appropriate, try showing your draft to a friend you trust and asking for their impressions.

Here is a bare-bones example:

Dear Rayna:
This is my formal notice that I will be resigning my position as account manager. My last day will be Friday, September 27.
   I appreciate the opportunities I have had at Fischl, and I have learned a great deal here. I wish you and team success in the future.
   Sincerely,
   Jeff

And now here's a different take on the same situation; this time, Jeff provides a bit more information, offers to help with the transition, and makes a point of wanting to stay in touch with Rayna:

Dear Rayna:

This is my formal notice that I will be resigning my position as account manager. My last day will be Friday, September 27. I have accepted a position at the Thompson Group and am looking forward to expanded responsibilities in my new role.

I would be happy to work with you during the transition and support the training for my replacement.

I appreciate the opportunities I have had at Fischl. I have learned a great deal from working with you and the team. I wish you all success in the future, and I hope we can stay in touch.

Sincerely,

Jeff

Termination Letters

Firing someone is never fun, but a well-written letter can make the process smoother for everyone and help protect you from a legal challenge.

A termination should be initiated in person and followed up by a formal letter, delivered either by hand or via certified mail. You should never fire an employee by e-mail. And it should go without saying that you should never fire anyone via social media. In addition to concerns about basic decency, doing so could expose you to accusations of wrongful termination or harassment.

If you work for a large organization, there are probably guidelines in place for termination procedures. Obviously, you should follow those scrupulously. If your organization doesn't have such guidelines and if you're concerned about whether you're handling the termination properly, you should consult an attorney for guidance.

BE CLEAR ABOUT YOUR PURPOSE

If writing a termination letter worries you, it might help to keep your objectives clearly in mind: to give formal notice to an employee that their employment is ending, to notify them of their last day of work, and to state the conditions of their termination. That's it—your letter does not need to do anything more.

CONSIDER YOUR READER

Putting yourself in the shoes of your reader can help guide you as you write. It's a fair bet that your reader won't be happy, but if you have had a conversation with her prior to writing the letter, she won't be surprised, either. Do your best to cushion the blow by remaining professional and courteous. Be fair, and allow the reader to maintain her dignity.

SAY IT RIGHT UP FRONT

The opening of your letter should mention the meeting you had with the employee, let him know that his employment is terminated, and note his final day of employment.

BE CAREFUL WHAT YOU SAY

The content of your letter should be factual, not emotional. You may feel disappointed, frustrated, or angry: don't show it. You may feel regretful or guilty: don't show that, either. Don't apologize. Any of these reactions can be used against you later if the employee decides to claim that she's been dismissed improperly or unfairly.

It's not always necessary to state the reasons for termination. However, when an employee is fired for cause, you might want to provide the reason for termination, as well as reviewing the steps that were taken to resolve the problem prior to the decision to terminate. If you do decide to discuss the reasons for termination, make sure they are consistent with what you've discussed with the employee earlier; otherwise you might risk a legal challenge. If you have any questions about whether you're handling this information properly, consult with HR or with legal counsel.

Your letter should answer all of the employee's questions about the termination: the effective date, the terms, any action the employee must take (returning keys, equipment, or badges, for example), and any benefits or pay due to the employee. You might also state the terms for verification of employment. Last, your letter should provide the employee with a contact in case they have any questions.

IF SOMETHING FEELS WRONG, FIX IT

It's important that you not send a termination letter before you've checked over it carefully. Double-check to make sure your tone is professional and businesslike and that you're showing no emotion. Make sure you're supplying all the information the employee needs to take the next steps. And ensure that you haven't left anything for the employee to grab hold of and use to raise a legal challenge to the termination.

Dear Sandra:

This letter confirms our discussion today that your employment with EverSold is terminated effective as of this date.

As we discussed in our meeting, the reason for the termination of your employment is poor attendance. You have missed a total of 18 workdays this calendar year, with no medical excuse. You were given written warnings on March 22 and April 17 of this year. During your performance review on June 7, I warned you that continued absence would result in termination. Nevertheless, you have missed work on several occasions since then, including June 12 and June 15, again with no medical excuse.

Payment for your accrued vacation days will be included in your final paycheck, which you will receive this Friday. You may pick up your check from the reception desk, or we can mail it to your home.

You will receive a separate benefits status letter that will outline the status of your benefits upon termination. The letter will include information about your eligibility for Consolidated Omnibus Budget Reconciliation Act (COBRA) continuation of group health coverage.

We have received from you your security swipe card and your office key at the termination meeting.

Sincerely,

Cara Bufalino

Resources

This section offers guidance on writing technique, style, grammar, and punctuation. It's not intended to be a comprehensive guide to any of these topics. Rather, it targets the most common errors in business writing and offers help with those areas where business writers struggle the most.

The English language is always changing, and the rules change along with it. Not everyone is aware of the rules, and not everyone cares. From a practical point of view, though, you should make an effort to use correct English when you write at work, for two reasons.

The first is that there are sticklers in every organization, with their eyes peeled for errors. Sometimes these people are powerful, and often they take pride in their knowledge of English. They can be a tremendous asset to an organization, but they can also be a pain in the neck and make you feel insecure about your writing. (It's worth pointing out that sometimes these people are wrong, and will "correct" you when you've done nothing wrong.) However you feel about these sticklers, you have to deal with them if you work with them, and having a solid understanding of grammar, usage, and style can boost your confidence and improve your writing.

The second, and better, reason that you should use correct English is that you really ought to care. If communication is part of your job, you should take pride in doing it well. In the end, it's not hard to learn the difference between the active and passive voices. It's not difficult to master the proper use of commas and semicolons. When you make the effort to get these kinds of things right in your writing, you'll see some interesting results in yourself. You'll feel more confident, you'll project that confidence, and you'll have greater impact through your writing.

WRITING SKILLS

Overcoming Writer's Block

Across various surveys I've conducted with business writers over the past twenty-five years, about 70 percent of them have reported experiencing writer's block. Writer's block hits most people at one time or another. When writer's block interferes with your productivity and leaves you staring at a blank screen, try these techniques to help yourself get started.

UNDERSTAND THE REASON

There's almost always an identifiable reason behind your writer's block. Often the most effective way to get yourself unblocked is to spend some time exploring *why* you feel you can't write. A very common reason is not being sure exactly what you want to say; maybe you need to spend some time brainstorming before you start to write. Another common reason is lack of confidence: you're worried that the finished product won't be any good. In this case, it might help to remember that your first draft is just that—a first draft—and no one but you will see it. Think hard about why you're feeling blocked, and you might just hit on a practical solution to the problem.

CLOSE THE DOOR

If you're feeling distracted by noise or activity nearby, try to arrange for a place and a time in which you won't be disturbed. Close your door, shut down your e-mail program and your web browser, turn off your phone, and tell your colleagues or your family you won't be available for a while. Having some private space and time can help you focus on your writing.

REWARD YOURSELF

Instead of running out for coffee before you write, try making that coffee (or a piece of chocolate or a trip to the gym—whatever you like) your reward for putting in some quality time on your writing project. It's easier to knuckle down when you know that you'll earn something you like for doing the work.

WRITE IT FOR YOUR GRANDMOTHER

Maybe worries about your reader's potential reaction are making it hard for you to get started. If that's the case, you can overcome your block by imagining a different reader—someone who's sympathetic to you, interested in what you have to say, and unlikely to judge you harshly: your grandmother. Get your writing process started by imagining that you are writing for your grandmother—or anyone else who's unconditionally kind. You'll make it clear and straightforward, and you won't dump a lot of jargon in. Once you have a draft, you can revise it to meet the more exacting standards of your actual reader.

WRITE IT BADLY

Are you convinced that your writing isn't going to be any good? Then instead of worrying about it, go ahead and write the whole thing as badly as you can. Write it ungrammatically; use inappropriate vocabulary. No one but you is going to see this draft, so go wild. Once you've got a bad draft, you can revise it into a good one, and you will have had some fun in the process.

Note: if you're trying this trick in an e-mail window, fill in the "to" field with your *own* e-mail address, not the intended recipient's, while you're working on your draft. It's easy to send off a draft by accident. To be extra safe, write your bad draft in a separate text file, then copy and paste into an e-mail when you're done revising.

WORK SOMEPLACE ELSE

If you get discouraged sitting in front of the computer, try writing someplace else. Grab pen and paper or your laptop and find an empty conference room. Try sitting in a coffee shop. Try jotting notes while you're on the bus or the train. Sometimes changing your environment will change your approach just enough to help you get your writing task under way.

Getting Your Writing Done Faster

> *"I have little time to plan my writing, and it generally takes a little while to perfect it. Time, as they say, is of essence."*
>
> —SURVEY RESPONDENT

Most of my clients tell me they need to get through their writing tasks faster. We're all pressed for time at work, and writing has become a critically important part of many jobs.

Here are a few tricks to help you write faster:

Use a template. If you do certain writing tasks frequently, take a few minutes to create a template that you can use over and over again. The point here is to avoid reinventing the wheel every time you write. Your template doesn't have to be fancy—even a quick outline can help you focus and get started. Refine the template as you continue to use it, to make it as efficient as possible.

Make a time for writing. Mark out a time in your day just for writing—for answering e-mails or working on any other writing tasks you're facing. It doesn't have to be the same time every day; it just has to be 100 percent dedicated to writing: no phone calls, no other interruptions. You can get a lot of writing done in twenty minutes if there are no other demands on that time.

Think before you write. It may seem counterintuitive, but taking some time to plan out what you're going to write can save you a tremendous amount of time in the long run.

When you start writing before you know what you want to say, you often end up spending more time later reworking and rewriting your text.

Finally, get into the habit of *proofreading* what you've written. Even the most experienced writers make more mistakes when they're in a hurry. It may take a few seconds to proofread your work, but catching errors before they reach others can save you a lot of time in cleaning up the confusion that can result from typos or muddy expression.

The Secret to Overcoming Writer's Block

Anita Campbell

When you're stuck, start talking. Literally. It's the fastest way I've found to get over writer's block.

I write a lot, each and every day. I used to struggle, staring at a blank screen. Sometimes getting that first paragraph down was the hardest part. Once I got going, it wasn't so bad to finish. But jeez Louise, pushing out that first paragraph was misery. As you can imagine, for someone like me—the publisher of an online journal—who communicates for a living, writer's block could seriously hamper my career.

How did I overcome it? My secret is simple: use voice dictation technology.

The past five years have seen huge advances in voice recognition and voice activation technologies. Voice recognition has become "intelligent," with predictive text corrections that amaze me. And the good news is that there are free applications out there, so you can experiment to see if voice dictation works for you, without fronting any money to buy software.

For example, did you know that Windows 10 has built-in voice dictation capabilities? I've used it to dictate into a WordPress site on a Windows PC. Microsoft also has an application called "Dictate," which uses its more advanced Cortana technology to let you dictate into Microsoft Office documents. Google Docs now features built-in voice typing, too (under the "Tools" menu). And various Apple devices enable dictation. However, some people who decide they like to dictate will opt for an advanced application, such as Dragon software.

Whatever your choice, here's a tip: don't try to edit immediately or clean up your first sentences as soon as you start dictating. At first, just get the words flowing. The goal is to get over the psychological hump. Once you have a few paragraphs dictated, then go back and edit your ramblings. At that point, you might even decide to switch to typing in order to finish the piece. By the time you get deep into whatever you're writing, the dictation has served its purpose. It got you over your initial writer's block. And that's what counts!

Anita Campbell is the founder, CEO, and publisher of Small Business Trends *(smallbiztrends.com) and its associated online publications, communities, and newsletters. She writes one thousand words a day.*

Editing Your Own Writing

Editing your own writing can be challenging. It's ideal to have someone else edit your work for you, but that's not always possible. These tips for self-editing will help you ensure that your writing is as accurate, complete, and concise as possible before you share it with the world.

TAKE A BREAK FROM YOUR WRITING

Taking a break from your writing can help you gain more perspective on it. If possible, leave your first draft overnight and return to it with a fresh eye the next day. If that's not possible, stand up from your desk for at least a few minutes and get your mind on something else before returning to your writing to edit. You'll find that the distance helps you see your draft more objectively.

PRETEND YOU'RE THE INTENDED READER

How will your reader react to your writing? One way to help answer this critical question is to imagine that *you* are the intended reader of the document as you review it. Put yourself in your reader's shoes. What's your response to the document? Is the purpose clear? If there's an action requested, do you know what it is and why? Is there any information missing? Is the tone appropriate? Imagining yourself as the recipient of the document can help you find areas for improvement.

READ IT OUT LOUD

Reading your draft out loud is an excellent way to catch problems in your writing, including missing words, awkward sentences, and incomplete thoughts. Find a quiet place, and listen as you read. Your final draft will be better for it.

WEED OUT UNNECESSARY WORDS

First drafts are often full of wordy constructions that can be trimmed. Go through your draft sentence by sentence and look for verbiage that isn't doing any work. Check out the examples below and see if you can make similar revisions in your own draft.

> **Original:** *Jackson is of the opinion that the restoration of the bases can be accomplished within six months or so.*
>
> **Revised:** *Jackson believes that the bases can be restored in about six months.*

Original: *In most circumstances, the practice of the committee is to weigh a variety of different options before arriving at a final decision.*

Revised: *The committee usually weighs different options before making a decision.*

PROOFREAD CAREFULLY

There's no substitute for careful proofreading. Don't trust spelling- or grammar-checking software to catch errors. These programs typically cannot find errors like the mistyping of "coed" for "code." And they have no way to "know" the correct spelling of many personal or product names. Ultimately, it's up to you to proofread your draft word by word to avoid any embarrassing mistakes.

FIX SLOW BEGINNINGS

A strong and specific beginning can engage readers and motivate them to keep reading. Use these tricks to help improve sentences that begin slowly, so that you'll get your readers involved right away.

* Look out for the **"blah blah blah is that"** sentence opening. Some writers feel they need to add some warm-up syllables to a sentence before they get to the point. Consider these common beginnings:

  > *The point is that . . .*
  > *It is important to remember that . . .*
  > *It is essential that . . .*
  > *The purpose of X is to Y . . .*

  Most of the time you can do without these and just get straight to the point.

* Look out for empty words. Phrases like the ones below creep into our writing without our realizing it, but they don't mean anything:

> *In many circumstances* . . . (How many? Are there really many, or is this just noise? If you mean "often," say "often.")
>
> *In many ways* . . . (How many ways? Look out for this one— it's usually just filler. If you can't answer the question "How many ways, and which ones?," you're probably just vamping.)
>
> *In order to* . . . (This almost always means just "to.")

Remember that readers may be skimming rather than reading, so it's important to place the key concepts where readers can see them easily. Sentences that begin with long introductory phrases are not incorrect or even poorly styled, but they do tend to push the important stuff toward the end.

Writing for Mobile Devices

Nearly everything you write might be read on a phone or a tablet. Website content marketers and copywriters have led the way in setting best practices for writing for mobile platforms. But now everything from e-mails to proposals is likely to be opened and read on a tablet or a phone. Writing with mobile devices in mind shouldn't be an afterthought; it should be a routine practice. The following tips can help ensure that what you write is easy to scan on a mobile screen.

Think visually. This one almost goes without saying, and it's the only thing you need to remember: envision how your content is going to look on a (much) smaller screen.

Consider that a single sentence can fill the entire screen of a phone. Long paragraphs can mean scrolling and scrolling. The ability to envision what your writing is going to look like on a phone screen or on a tablet is the cornerstone of writing for mobile.

Front-load your content. The more a reader has to scroll, the more likely that reader is to give up and go do something else. Make sure you get your most important content right up front. Even if you have to develop that content more fully later in the document, make sure you get your main ideas out there in front.

Be concise. Writing concisely is a virtue no matter what delivery method you use, but on mobile screens it's a live-or-die matter. Long sentences, complex constructions, and extra words will make your reader's experience unnecessarily laborious.

Format for ease of scanning. When you're writing for ordinary screens or for printing, you want to use formatting—paragraph breaks, headings, bullet points, bolding—to make your content easier to scan. That's even more important for mobile platforms. Imagine that you've written a proposal that your potential customer is viewing on his phone. If he starts reading a prose paragraph, he's got no idea how long it's going to be, because he can't see the whole thing. He might find himself scrolling and scrolling through a long paragraph and beginning to feel lost. You can help him with these formatting practices:

* Use headlines to orient the reader.
* Use bulleted or numbered lists where appropriate.
* Write short sentences and short paragraphs.

> Buddhists believe that there is only the present. The past is gone, and the future is uncertain; all we have for sure is now. You should adopt the same kind of thinking when you're writing for mobile platforms. On a mobile device, a reader can't see a full document, and she can't see the larger context—all she's got is the screen in front of her. It's your job as a writer to ensure that your content is communicated effectively on the mobile platform.

STYLE

Active Voice—Make Your Writing More Direct

The grammatical term "voice" refers to whether the subject of the sentence acts or receives the action. If the subject is doing the acting, the sentence is in the active voice ("Joe kicks the ball"); if the subject is acted upon, the sentence is in the passive voice ("The ball is kicked by Joe"). The passive voice is made up of a form of the verb "to be" and the past participle of another verb (e.g., "is eaten," "are preferred," "was chosen," or "were stolen").

Writers in many different settings tend to overuse the passive voice, and the result is often lackluster, vague writing.

COMMON REASONS FOR USING THE PASSIVE VOICE

To avoid taking responsibility ("We didn't do it; it just *happened*.")

> Our fees for services *were increased*.

> An error *was made* in calculating your statement.

To sound authoritative

> The decision *was investigated* and *was found* to be sound.

To hedge

> The project *is expected* to be completed on time.
>
> No inconvenience to the occupants *is anticipated*.

BETTER REASONS FOR USING THE PASSIVE VOICE

You don't know the actor or you prefer not to identify him or her

> The fire alarm *was set off* over the weekend.

You want to emphasize the object of the action rather than the actor

> The report *was prepared* by Terry Monroe.
>
> (Where the emphasis is on the report, not on Terry.)
>
> The new assistant *was recommended* by Jody McCarron.
>
> (Where the emphasis is on the assistant, not on Jody.)

TRANSFORMING PASSIVE CONSTRUCTIONS INTO ACTIVE ONES

Transforming passive constructions into active constructions is easy, and the resulting sentences are usually shorter, more direct, more specific, and more interesting. To change a passive construction into an active one, identify the person or thing that is doing the action, make it the subject of the sentence, and continue with any necessary alterations. You may find that the actor isn't present in the sentence at all; in that case, figure out what it is and insert it.

> Passive: *The speaker was ignored by the audience for most of the presentation.*
>
> Active: *The audience ignored the speaker for most of the presentation.*
>
> Passive: *The ship was prepared for launch by its crew.*
>
> Active: *The ship's crew prepared it for launch.*

Passive: *The novel was judged to be one of the best of the decade.*
(The actor is missing from this sentence.)
Active: *Critics judged the novel to be one of the best of the decade.*

Using a passive construction is *not* incorrect. In general, however, active constructions are more interesting and engaging to read. Becoming adept at using the passive and active voices will help you become a stronger and more skilled writer.

(For more about voice, please see Step 4.)

Reading, Writing, and Leadership
Jerry Reece

President Harry Truman once famously said, "Not all readers are leaders, but all leaders are readers." This statement certainly rings true, as influential leaders from the past, including President Teddy Roosevelt and Sir Winston Churchill, frequently traveled around the world with their libraries at their disposal.

I had the pleasure of meeting Alfred W. Tatum, PhD—the dean of the College of Education at the University of Illinois at Chicago. Dr. Tatum informed me that he uses a scale to make sure he reads five pounds of books per month. I have personally adopted this practice and encourage everyone who has leadership aspirations to read a lot, not just in their chosen fields but broadly across all topics.

However, I would take President Truman's thought one step further and assert that *not all writers are leaders, but all leaders are writers*. Communication is the single most important key to leadership success. In all lines of business, the ability to effectively and persuasively write and communicate is what propels the great leaders above their peers.

In real estate, for example, you must be able to clearly, concisely, and efficiently convey your client's intentions in written contracts without ambiguity; otherwise, deals are lost, and clients will leave you. To build a successful real estate career, it is not enough simply to be a good salesperson. You must also be able to translate what you say you can do into skillfully written documents so you can successfully close the deal.

In today's fast-paced business world, strong reading and writing habits are more important than ever to the development of leadership skills. No amount of tech savvy can replace the critical thinking skills built through reading and writing, and the amount of "noise" in the environment makes clear communication even more important. The libraries we carry with us now may be on our iPads rather than in printed books, but the top business leaders still read widely and prioritize strong written communication.

Jerry Reece is chairman emeritus of ReeceNichols, a leader in real estate in the Kansas City area.

This What?

Here's a quick and easy trick to help you cultivate a more engaging writing style: avoid using the word "this" as a stand-alone subject. "This" can be used in two ways.

As a demonstrative pronoun: *This is difficult.*
Or as an adjective: *This project is difficult.*

When used as a pronoun, "this" stands in the place of a noun. In a sentence like "This is difficult," you can assume that, from the context, people know what "this" means. It's a little harder to follow, however, when you try to use the pronoun "this" to stand in for something more complex than a simple idea. Let's look at an example:

We might improve the process by having the prep team notify AK when the first phase has been completed. This would allow AK to prepare to move the product to phase two. This could eliminate an entire step of the HD process.

In the second and third sentences above, what do you figure "this" means? This what? In these sentences, "this" is being asked to do too much, and the result is vague, weak prose. Let's look at a revision:

We might improve the process by having the prep team notify AK when the first phase been completed. AK could then prepare early to move the product to phase two. Setting up this kind of notification system could eliminate an entire step of the HD process.

The revision is more specific and easier to follow. Is it possible for a reader to guess what the original version means? Probably. Is it better not to make the reader guess? Certainly.

When you're about to use "this" to stand in for a complex idea, take a moment to write out what you mean explicitly. If you have trouble doing so, it's a sign that you were "cheating" a little bit and expecting that little word to do the hard work you didn't want to do. Taking the trouble to think through exactly what you mean will help guide your reader and make your point more clearly.

Gender-Neutral Language

The English language has gendered pronouns in the third person— that is, "he" and "she." Once upon a time, the masculine pronouns "he," "him," "his," and "himself" were considered acceptable for use as gender-neutral pronouns in situations where the sex of the person was not known:

> *Everyone should lock his office door at the end of the day.*
> *The successful executive has confidence, and he can communicate effectively with everyone.*
> *A worker is only as good as his tools.*
> *Modern man no longer coddles himself during pregnancy. He continues to work often until days before he goes into labor and delivers.*

That last example calls into question the neutrality of the pronoun, doesn't it? Today, the masculine pronoun is no longer considered gender-neutral, which leaves professional writers with some choices to make when they want to be inclusive. No one has yet developed a widely accepted gender-neutral English pronoun, so we're left with a few different options when we want to write without specifying the gender of the person we're talking about.

USE "HE OR SHE" OR "SHE OR HE"

The phrases "he or she" or "she or he" can work, especially if used sparingly. This construction can be clunky when it's used in situations where the pronoun appears more than once in a single sentence:

> *Everyone should lock his or her office door at the end of the day.*

But not:

> *Everyone should lock his or her office door at the end of the day and ensure that he or she turns off the copier and printer.*

USE S/HE AND HIS/HER

This option is typographically more efficient than using "she or he," but it reads unnaturally:

The successful executive has confidence, and s/he can communicate effectively with everyone.

ALTERNATE USING "HE" AND "SHE"

If you have a fairly long text that features a lot of pronouns, you can alternate using "he" and "she," showing equal favor to both. That's the primary approach chosen for this book. However, it won't work if you have a string of sentences that require the pronoun; the alternation will seem bizarre and confusing.

USE "THEY" AND "THEIR" AS SINGULAR PRONOUNS

Many writers use "they" and "their" to refer back to a singular subject, when the gender of that subject is unknown:

Everyone should lock their office door at the end of the day.
Somebody got their handprints all over the bathroom mirror; they ought to go back and clean it off.

Sticklers and traditionalists will point out that this construction is grammatically incorrect, because "everyone" is singular and "their" is plural. They're right, and you should be aware that some readers won't approve of this solution to the gender-neutral challenge. However, it's an approach that many, if not most, people have adopted in everyday speech. There are examples of "they" used as a singular pronoun going back as far as the fourteenth century, and it was only in the nineteenth century that grammarians began to object to it. For us twenty-first-century types, using "they" as a singular pronoun is probably all right in most settings; in very formal writing, it might be smart to find another alternative.

PLURALIZE YOUR SENTENCE

Instead of making a plural work as a singular, and possibly alienating some readers, consider pluralizing the whole sentence:

Successful executives have confidence, and they can communicate
effectively with everyone.
Workers are only as good as their tools.

Rewrite the Sentence to Avoid Using Third-Person Pronouns

Sometimes the best solution is to rewrite the sentence without third-person pronouns. This approach is always safe:

Please lock your office door at the end of the day.
Whoever got handprints all over the mirror should go back and
clean it up.

Be Consistent

Whatever option you choose, be sure you implement it consistently; don't switch from one style to another in midstream.

Not:

The new STEP app allows users to choose what action to take once
he/she logs in.

But:

The new STEP app allows users to choose what action to take once
they log in.

Or:

The new STEP app allows each user to choose what action to take
once he/she logs in.

GRAMMAR AND USAGE

Sentences, Fragments, and Run-ons

The sentence is the basic building block of writing. Fragments and run-ons masquerade as sentences, but they're incorrect and often confusing. For clarity and correctness, you're wise to use proper sentences in formal and informal writing.

SENTENCES

A sentence contains a subject and a verb and expresses a complete thought.

The subject of a sentence is a noun or pronoun that names a person, place, or thing: "the committee," "Justin," "she," "they," "Scotland," "the backyard," "Wall Street," "the laptop," "a cat," "a regulation."

It can also be a series of words that function as a noun, because they name a thing: "running the application."

A verb is a word that expresses action or a state of being: "provide," "argue," "is," "are," "were."

To be considered a sentence, a group of words must have both a subject and a verb:

The committee provides guidelines for the implementation of each stage.
They argue a lot, but they never get anywhere.
The laptop is broken.

FRAGMENTS

A fragment is an incomplete sentence. It's usually missing its subject or its verb. It hints at a complete thought but does not express it. For example:

Ran the backup overnight.
Not a full-blown detailed blueprint.

Run-ons

A run-on sentence is two or more sentences stuck together without a conjunction (like "and" or "but") or appropriate punctuation (like a semicolon).

> *Everyone came in for the meeting, there was no place to sit.*
> *There's not much content under the first bullet maybe we should add a line or two.*

Here are two easy ways to fix these run-ons:

> *Everyone came in for the meeting, **but** there was no place to sit.*
> *There's not much content under the first bullet, **so** maybe we should add a line or two.*

Or:

> *There's not much content under the first bullet; maybe we should add a line or two.*

Pronoun Pitfalls

Pronouns are words that stand in for nouns. They can take different forms depending on what part they play in a sentence. Personal pronouns used as subjects take the **nominative case**: "I," "you," "he," "she," "we," and "they." Personal pronouns used as direct or indirect objects, or as objects of a preposition, take the **objective case**: "me," "you," "him," "her," "us," and "them." Most of the time, writers use pronouns correctly. However, there are a few common errors you should beware.

Not:

> *Please send the finished reviews to George and **I**.*

But:

*Please send the finished reviews to George and **me**.*

If alarm bells are going off in your head right now, it's probably because you can hear your mother's voice exclaiming, "George and I!" She was saying that because you said, "George and me are going to ride bikes," or maybe "Me and George are going to ride bikes." She was trying to get you to use the nominative case of the pronoun as the subject of the sentence, and she was right. In this case, however, you need the objective case. "George" and "me" are objects of the preposition "to," so you need the objective case, even if it sounds weird.

How do you know? In this case, simply drop "George and" and see how it sounds:

*Please send the finished reviews to **I**.*

You can tell that's wrong. It's wrong because you need "me," in the objective case, as the object of the preposition "to." So it needs to be "George and me." By the same token, you can now probably see that this sentence is incorrect:

*The work was divided between **he and I**.*

Instead, you need pronouns in the objective case as objects of the preposition "between":

*The work was divided between **him and me**.*

Another common pronoun problem is the incorrect use of **reflexive pronouns**. The reflexive form of the pronoun contains the word "self." Think of the form **reflecting** back on itself: "myself," "yourself," "himself," "herself," "ourselves," and "themselves." Reflexive pronouns are used only to refer to another word in the sentence or to emphasize another word in the sentence.

*I hurt **myself**.*
*She did all the coding **herself**.*

Reflexive pronouns like "myself" never stand alone. So common constructions like this are incorrect:

*All the results will be reviewed by Loren and **myself**.*
*For people like **myself**, keeping up with technology can be difficult.*

In both of these cases, "myself" is not referring to another word in the sentence; hence the usage is incorrect. People use "myself" in this way in an attempt to sound more formal and more polite, but it's simply wrong. Those sentences should read:

*All the results will be reviewed by Loren and **me**.*
*For people like **me**, keeping up with technology can be difficult.*

Those versions might not sound fancy, but they're grammatically correct.

A third common pronoun controversy has to do with using "they" as a singular pronoun. Of course, "they" is plural form. But in order to avoid sexist writing, people have increasingly been using forms of "they" as a gender-neutral singular pronoun.

*Everyone should bring **their** own lunch.*
*We should let the assistant know when **they** will be needed.*

There's still some disagreement about whether this usage is acceptable in modern English, although more and more people (including me) consider it just fine. For a fuller discussion of this issue, see "Gender-Neutral Language" on page 201.

Misplaced and Dangling Modifiers

"Modifiers" are parts of speech that change, or modify, the meaning of other words. Adjectives modify nouns or pronouns (*the **silent** machine; the **rude** neighbor; she was **busy***). Adverbs modify verbs, adjectives, or other adverbs (*the machine ran **silently**; the report was **especially** dense; she spoke **very** quickly*).

Modifiers don't have to be single words. They can also be phrases:

*The heater **under the desk** was set on low.* (The phrase "under the desk" works as an adjective modifying "heater.")
*The operation ran **for a year** without full staffing.* (The phrase "for a year" functions as an adverb modifying "ran.")

As a general rule, modifiers should be placed as close as possible to the words they modify, to avoid confusion. A **misplaced modifier** is positioned in such a way that it's not clear what word it's supposed to modify. You might not notice a misplaced modifier at first, but once you do, the result is often nonsensical.

Not:

*The caterer served tostadas to the guests **on mini tortillas**.* (The guests were not on the tortillas, the tostadas were.)

But:

*The caterer served tostadas **on mini tortillas** to the guests.*

Or:

*The caterer served the guests tostadas **on mini tortillas**.*

Not:

*They brought an Italian chair for the new CEO **with an extra-wide seat**.* (Presumably it's the chair, not its occupant, that has the big seat.)

But:

*They brought an Italian chair **with an extra-wide seat** for the CEO.*

Not:

Working through the weekend, the presentation was finished by Monday. (It sounds like the presentation itself was working, not the people.)

But:

Working through the weekend, the team finished the presentation by Monday.

The most common misplaced modifier in the English language is probably "only."

Not:

*I **only** ate two doughnuts.* (This sentence suggests that you only ate them—you didn't play tennis with them or take them to a movie or pile them on your desk.)

But:

*I ate **only** two doughnuts.* (Remarkable self-restraint.)

Lots of readers won't notice the difference, but if you want to write correctly, it's worth being careful where you place "only" in a sentence.

A **dangling modifier** is a word that modifies another word that's not present in the sentence. You might guess at the meaning of the sentence, but dangling modifiers can result in confusion.

Not:

> *As one of my valued customers, I'm pleased to announce special loyalty prices for the month of September.* (As written, the sentence suggests that the writer is one of her own customers.)

But:

> *As one of my valued customers, you are eligible for special loyalty prices in the month of September.*

Not:

> *Hoping to impress the client, the baseball tickets were left with his assistant.* (As written, the sentence suggests that the tickets were hoping to impress the client. The person who was hoping is missing from the sentence altogether.)

But:

> *Hoping to impress the client, she left the baseball tickets with his assistant.*

Not:

> *Although majoring in business, Greg's interests also included world history and Asian languages.* (As written, the sentence suggests that Greg's "interests" are majoring in business, not Greg himself.)

But:

Although Greg was majoring in business, his interests also included world history and Asian languages.

"That" and "Which"

When to use "that" and when to use "which"—it's a mystery to a lot of business writers, but the answer is pretty easy to remember. "That" and "which" often introduce clauses. Clauses can be restrictive or nonrestrictive. A **restrictive** clause is essential to the meaning of the sentence:

*The room **that has the video screen** is already booked.*

In this example, "that has the video screen" defines the room you're talking about. Dropping that clause would cause the sentence to lose its meaning; it would no longer be clear which room is booked.

A **nonrestrictive** clause is not essential to the meaning of a sentence. If it's deleted, the sentence still makes sense and retains its meaning.

*Room 511, **which has a video screen**, seats twenty-five people.*

In this example, you can drop the clause and the sentence will still retain its meaning. The clause is nonrestrictive.

As you might infer from the examples above, "that" is used with restrictive clauses, and "which" is used with nonrestrictive clauses.

Not:

*I left my phone in the rental car **which I picked up in Memphis**.*

But:

*I left my phone in the rental car **that I picked up in Memphis**.*

This clause is restrictive. It's essential to the meaning of the sentence, so you need to introduce it with "that." It wasn't the car you picked up in Atlanta or the one you picked up in Cleveland; it was the one you picked up in Memphis.

On the other hand:

> *The rental car,* **which I picked up in Memphis,** *got two flat tires on the way over the bridge.*

The point of this sentence is that the car got two flat tires on the bridge. The fact that you picked it up in Memphis doesn't matter. It's a nonrestrictive clause, so it's introduced with "which."

It's worth noting that this rule exists only in American English, not in British English.

Split Infinitives

The **infinitive** form of a verb is the form that includes "to": "to run," "to understand," "to process," and so on. It's called an "infinitive" because it exists outside of time—that is, it's not in the present, past, or future tense. It's the base form of the verb.

A split infinitive is one where someone has inserted a word between the "to" and the main part of the verb. The world's most famous split infinitive comes from the original series of *Star Trek*, where Captain Kirk describes the mission of the *Enterprise*: "To boldly go where no man has gone before."

Many of us were taught that it's incorrect to split an infinitive. The reason for this is complicated and probably not interesting unless you're a big fan of grammatical history. All you need to know is that there are people out there, perhaps in your office, who feel that split infinitives are bad grammar and that you should avoid them. In response, you can do one of two things: (1) ignore these colleagues and risk being dinged for bad writing, or (2) try to avoid splitting infinitives.

If you choose the second course, consider moving the modifier to another place in the sentence. Often this solution works very well:

To boldly go where no man has gone before → *Boldly to go where no man has gone before*
To better understand the problem → *To understand the problem better*
To unilaterally reject the deal → *To reject the deal unilaterally*
We need to first explore the cheaper option → *First we need to explore the cheaper option*

Ending a Sentence with a Preposition

Many people will tell you that it's incorrect to end a sentence with a preposition. Others will tell you it's not a rule at all. If you're writing with the sticklers in mind, you'll want to avoid this practice.

There are several ways to rewrite a sentence that ends with a preposition.

For the next quarter, we need to decide which initiative to focus on.

Use "on which":

For the next quarter, we need to decide on which initiative to focus.

This solution can be awkward, as you can see, but sometimes it works well.

Reorder the sentence in another way:

We need to decide which initiative to focus on for the next quarter.

Find another word to replace the prepositional form:

For the next quarter, we need to decide which initiative to prioritize.

This rewrite sounds stronger than the initial version. Forms that contain a verb and a preposition can often be replaced with a single, stronger verb.

Talk about → *discuss*
Mull over → *consider*
Try out → *test*

"Unique"

"Unique" means "one of a kind." Don't use it to mean "special" or "distinctive." And don't use qualifiers like "very" with "unique." How could something be "very one of a kind"?

"Would Have," "Could Have"

The way most Americans speak, these terms sound a lot like "would of" and "could of." Be careful to write them correctly.

Not: *We **would of** gone if we had been there.*
But: *We **would have** gone if we had been there.*

COMMONLY CONFUSED WORDS

The English language has a lot of words that sound similar. It's easy to confuse them, especially when you're writing in a hurry. This list covers some of the most commonly confused words in the language; keep it handy to avoid mistakes.

Accept and **except**
Accept means to receive.
Except means apart from, otherwise than.

Adverse and averse

Adverse means harmful or unfavorable.

Averse means opposed to or strongly disinclined.

Affect and effect

To *affect* is to have an influence on or to create strong emotions.

An *effect* is a result or an outcome.

All right

All right means acceptable or in good order.

There is no such word as *alright*. It's a misspelling of *all right*.

All together and altogether

All together (two words) indicates people or things located in one place.

Altogether means completely, entirely.

Appraise and apprise

Appraise means to estimate the value of.

Apprise means to notify.

Chord and cord

A *chord* is a combination of musical notes sounded together.

A *cord* is a slender length of flexible material.

Note: It's *vocal cords,* NOT *vocal chords.*

Cite, site, sight

To *cite* is to refer to something, to note as a reference.

A *site* is a place, either real (e.g., a construction site) or virtual (e.g., a website).

A *sight* is something you see, like the Pyramids (a popular *sightseeing* destination) or a small child after finger painting ("You're a *sight!*").

Compliment and *complement*

A *compliment* is a comment of praise, admiration, or approval.

To *complement* something is to accompany it or complete it.

Conscience and *conscious*

Conscience means a sense of right and wrong.

Conscious refers to an alert mental state or a sense of awareness.

Elicit and *illicit*

Elicit means to draw forth or evoke.

Illicit means unlawful.

Imply and *infer*

To *imply* is to hint at something without saying it explicitly.

To *infer* is to draw a conclusion, to reason through deduction.

Its and *it's*

Its is a possessive form: *The house lost its roof in the storm.*

It's is a contraction of *it is*: *It's very cold out today.*

Pour and *pore*

To *pour* is to dispense a liquid.

To *pore* is to study something closely.

Note: You don't *pour* over a document, unless you're trying to get it wet. You *pore* over it.

Precede and *proceed*

To *precede* is to come before something in time, rank, or importance.

To *proceed* is to move forward or continue.

Principle and *principal*

A *principle* is a guiding belief or truth.

A *principal* is a governing officer in an organization (like a school or a firm).

Stationary and *stationery*

Stationary means fixed in one place, motionless.

Stationery refers to writing materials, especially envelopes and writing paper.

Their, there, and *they're*

Their indicates possession: *their car, their* philosophy, *their* problems.

There indicates a place or point: *The house is there. Start reading there.*

They're is a contraction of *they are*: *They're on vacation. They're under arrest.*

Through, threw, and *thorough*

Through indicates movement into one side and out another.

Threw is the past tense of *throw*.

Thorough means carried through to completion, complete, or careful about detail.

To, two, and *too*

To means in the direction, as far as.

Two is the number 2.

Too means *also*. It's also used as an intensifier: *too hot, too difficult.*

Your and *you're*

Your indicates possession: *your book, your office, your health.*

You're is a contraction of *you are*: *you're busy, you're right.*

PUNCTUATION

How to Use a Comma

Commas are the most frequently used punctuation marks, as well as the ones that cause the greatest confusion. Learning a few rules can boost your comma confidence.

USE A COMMA WHEN JOINING TWO FULL SENTENCES
WITH *AND, OR, BUT, SO, NOR,* OR *FOR.*
The flight was delayed, and they spent the night in a hotel.
Jennifer worked for the agency, but I never knew her there.
Almost everyone is here, so I think we should get started.
They have not upgraded this year, nor do they expect to upgrade next year.
Opening another plant in France was impossible, for the costs were too high.

USE A COMMA BETWEEN ITEMS IN A
SERIES. (NOTE THAT THESE ITEMS CAN
BE SINGLE WORDS OR PHRASES.)
The movers packed up the books, dishes, and artwork.
On Saturday we do the laundry, mow the lawn, and wash the car.
She enjoys playing the violin, working in the garden, and trading stock options.

Note: In these examples, the comma before the "and" is optional. Known as a "serial comma" or "Oxford comma," it is not required, but it can improve the clarity of a sentence.

USE A COMMA AFTER A LONG
INTRODUCTORY PHRASE OR CLAUSE.
With the surgery behind him, Tim was able to travel to Italy comfortably.

Because of the shortage of housing in the city, they moved to the suburbs.

USE A COMMA AFTER AN INTRODUCTORY ADVERB THAT MODIFIES THE ENTIRE SENTENCE.
Unfortunately, the guacamole was gone when they arrived.
Alternatively, we could take the train into the city.
On the other hand, it might be better to work on the taxes in the morning.

USE A COMMA TO SET OFF A NONRESTRICTIVE MODIFIER OR APPOSITIVE.
(An *appositive* is a noun or a pronoun set next to another to explain or identify it. A *nonrestrictive* element is not essential to the meaning of a sentence. If it's deleted, the sentence still makes sense and retains its meaning.)

The car, a black Lexus, was parked in the underground garage.
The sweater, which was too small already, shrank in the wash.

USE A COMMA TO SET OFF SENTENCE MODIFIERS AND SENTENCE ELEMENTS OUT OF THE NORMAL WORD ORDER.
The new software, unfortunately, is even harder to use than the old version.
Urban living, I think, will become the norm soon.

Note: Although it's tempting to insert a comma wherever you might pause in speech, you're far safer to follow the rules above than to punctuate "by ear."

How to Use Colons and Semicolons

Colons and semicolons frequently cause confusion, but they are very easy to master. The few rules explained here will equip you to use colons and semicolons correctly.

COLONS ARE USED TO *INTRODUCE*

Use a colon to introduce a list of things:

> *He bought all the ingredients for the recipe: pasta, tomato sauce, fresh tomatoes, and cheese.*

You can use a colon to introduce an entire sentence, if the second part explains the first.

> *The renovation was extensive: they replaced all the electrical and plumbing systems in the building.*

Think of a colon as saying "the following" or "in other words."

SEMICOLONS ARE USED TO *SEPARATE*

Use a semicolon when joining two full sentences *without* a conjunction like *and, or, but, nor,* or *for.*

> *Tony took the train home; Paul had a car.*
> *The dinner was great; the concert was disappointing.*

Use a semicolon when joining two full sentences with an adverb like *however* or *nevertheless.*

> *I finished the project on time; however, the office was closed when I went to deliver it.*
> *We asked them not to share the proposal with others; nevertheless, they circulated it to the whole team.*

Use semicolons to separate items in a series that themselves contain commas.

The publisher was looking for titles in project management, IT, and systems analysis; general management, leadership, and coaching; and computer literacy, the Internet, and web design.

How to Use Parentheses, Brackets, and Dashes

Many people use dashes, parentheses, and brackets interchangeably; however, each of these punctuation marks has its own correct usage. These guidelines will help you understand and use them correctly.

PARENTHESES

Use parentheses to enclose a loosely related comment, explanation, or elaboration within a sentence or a paragraph. You should be able to omit the material within the parentheses without changing the basic meaning or structure of the sentence or paragraph.

We saw a production of Titus Andronicus *(one of Shakespeare's earliest plays) in London.*
The cook (it was his first day on the job) used the wrong sauce for the enchiladas.
Al worked for the National Transportation Safety Board (NTSB) in Washington, D.C.

Note: A parenthetical sentence within another sentence has no initial capital letter or period.

At that point all flights were canceled. (The rain had gotten much heavier.) We had no choice but to wait.

Note: A freestanding parenthetical sentence requires an initial capital letter and a period inside the parentheses.

BRACKETS

Use brackets to indicate that you have inserted something into a quotation to clarify the meaning.

> *Deb said during her acceptance speech, "I am honored by it [the award], but I could not have achieved this without the help of my staff."*

You can also use brackets to set off an interpolation *within* parentheses.

> *By a vote of 5–4, the Supreme Court overturned the lower court's ruling. (See page 153 [Figure A] for a chronology of the case.)*

DASHES

Use dashes to indicate a break in thought.

> *The truth is—and you probably already know it—that we can't manage without you.*
> *I think we can go ahead and accept—no, we can't!*

You can also use a dash to introduce a summary or explanation.

> *It was a close call—the sudden wind almost overturned the boat.*
> *Legislators were in a tough position—they had to fund the program without raising taxes.*
> (Colons can also be used for this purpose.)

How to Use Capital Letters

Capitalization often seems arbitrary, probably because so many people use capitals incorrectly. Everyone knows to capitalize the first letter of a sentence and people's names; the following few rules will help you capitalize correctly every time.

CAPITALIZE ALL THE WORDS IN PLACE-NAMES

Silver Lake, Park Avenue, Atlantic Ocean, Appalachian Mountains, Pacific Coast Highway, Atwater Village, New York City

CAPITALIZE RECOGNIZED SECTIONS OF THE WORLD OR THE COUNTRY

the South, the Sunset Strip, the Northwest, the Lake District, the Far East

DON'T CAPITALIZE *EAST, WEST, NORTH,* OR *SOUTH* WHEN THEY INDICATE DIRECTION; DO CAPITALIZE THEM WHEN THEY REFER TO RECOGNIZED SECTIONS OF A COUNTRY

Go west on Colorado Boulevard till you hit the freeway.
Just east of the house, there's a stand of eucalyptus trees.
the Midwest, the West Coast, the Southeast, the Northeast, the West Country

CAPITALIZE THE NAMES OF ORGANIZATIONS, BUSINESSES, INSTITUTIONS, AND GOVERNMENT BODIES

League of Women Voters, National Geographic Society, Delta Air Lines, Plaza Hotel, Columbia University, National Science Foundation, Department of English and Comparative Literature, House of Representatives, Federal Aviation Administration, Internal Revenue Service

CAPITALIZE THE NAMES OF HISTORICAL EVENTS AND PERIODS, SPECIAL EVENTS, AND CALENDAR ITEMS

Civil War, Renaissance, Kentucky Derby, Special Olympics, Monday, June, Halloween, Memorial Day, Administrative Professionals' Week

CAPITALIZE THE NAMES OF SHIPS, PLANES, MONUMENTS, AND AWARDS

the Merrimac, *the* Spruce Goose, *the Vietnam Memorial, the Academy Awards, the Statue of Liberty*

CAPITALIZE THE TITLES OF BOOKS, STORIES, POEMS, SONGS, MOVIES, AND OTHER WORKS OF ART

The Hobbit, The Red Badge of Courage, The Big Sleep, Paradise Lost, *"The Raven," "Twist and Shout," "I Wanna Be Sedated,"* Lawrence of Arabia, Star Trek

WHAT NOT TO CAPITALIZE

Do not capitalize a word just because the concept seems important to you (a really annoying habit known among editors as Very Important Thing syndrome).

How to Use Quotation Marks

Quotation marks are used to set off words in a sentence. Most frequently, they indicate a direct quotation from someone other than the writer. Quotation marks are frequently misused, but if you learn these few rules you'll never go wrong.

DOUBLE QUOTATION MARKS

In American usage, you'll need double quotation marks, not single ones, most of the time. You'll need to use single quotation marks if you have a quotation within a quotation.

Penelope told us what happened in the meeting: "Marc and Jen both said, 'This is a really terrible idea' at the same time."

Use quotation marks to set off the exact words of a speaker or writer.

Gail read the message and blurted out, "That's ridiculous."
The sign over the door said, "No bicycles or skateboards."

Use quotation marks for the titles of articles, essays, poems, chapters, and songs. (Titles of books, magazines, and newspapers belong in italics. Here, because the example sentences are set in italics, those titles reverse out to roman.)

His song "Let's Call the Whole Thing Off" appeared in the 1937 movie Shall We Dance.
Her essay "Shakespeare's Language" was reprinted in the book Renaissance Literary Rhetoric.

Use quotation marks to indicate the ironic use of a word.

One of the "advantages" the broker mentioned was the apartment's proximity to a punk rock club.

Use quotation marks to refer to a word being used as the word itself.

The word "pizza" first appeared in a Latin text in the year 997.

Don't use quotation marks to add emphasis. Use italics, boldface, or underlining instead, and do so only sparingly.

Not like this:

Food is "not" permitted in the theater.

Like this:

*Food is **not** permitted in the theater.*

Not like this:

"No" parking during business hours.

Like this:

Absolutely no parking during business hours.

Punctuation with Quotation Marks
Commas and periods go *inside* the quotation marks.*

"I'm sure," said Joe, "that we'll be done with this project by Friday."

Exclamation points and question marks go inside the quotation marks when they are part of the quotation.

"Holy cats!" she said. "Is this project ever going to end?"

Semicolons and colons go *outside* the quotation marks.

The judge commented that the mortgage company had behaved "unconscionably"; the plaintiff's motion was upheld.
He was described as "the quintessential team player": focused, cooperative, and supportive of his colleagues.

---

* This is American usage. British usage is different.

Acknowledgments

Many people have helped in the writing of this book, through reading and reviewing sections of it, making suggestions, generally teaching me about business communication, and supporting my work in different ways. My deep thanks to Gail J. Anderson, Lisa Curry Austin, Penelope Boehm, Professor Ming-Jer Chen, Robert C. Daugherty, Alex Egan, Alan Fierstein, Catherine M. Gleason, Heidi J. Holder, Jen Kruper, Glenn Leibowitz, Byron Loyd, Karina Mikucka, Syed Mohiuddin, Jill Niemczyk Murphy, Fred Null, Alison Paddock, Steven Paddock, Rex B. Posadas, Steven Schwarz, Halvar Trodahl, and Marc Zegans. Special thanks to Stephanie Walls, whose conscientiousness, ace problem-solving skills, and good humor have cleared many obstacles from my path.

The dedicatee, Catherine M. Rose, was my English teacher during my seventh and eighth grade years and has been an important person in my life ever since. Ms. Rose inspired in me—and in many of her other students—a lifelong love of good writing and great literature. Much of the advice you'll read in this book came to me first from Cathy, and I'm very grateful to her for setting the groundwork for much of my career.

I'm also indebted to the contributors to this book for sharing their special expertise on a variety of business writing topics. The wisdom they've shared from their fascinating careers enriches the book tremendously. You can read about them and their expertise in the "Contributors" section (page 237) and enjoy their insights throughout the book.

Deep gratitude is due to my agent, Jim Levine, of Levine Greenberg

Rostan and my editor at W. W. Norton, Jill Bialosky. Thank you both for the opportunities and support.

My author photo was taken by the late and much beloved Arthur Cohen.

Appendix A:
Business Writing Survey

This survey was conducted from April through August 2016. It was piloted with a group of my associates. Then it was promoted initially among my clients and associates and later on Facebook, Twitter, and LinkedIn. Survey respondents were entered into a contest to win a copy of *How to Write Anything: A Complete Guide* (W. W. Norton, 2014). Five winners were selected and the books distributed. There were 528 responses in total.

Survey Questions

1. **How important is writing in your workplace?**
   Please answer using a five-point scale where 1 is "not important at all" and 5 is "very important."

   > 1   2   3   4   5

2. **What kinds of things do you write most often at work?**
   (Check as many as you wish.)
   - ○ E-mails
   - ○ Requests
   - ○ Proposals
   - ○ Formal letters
   - ○ Reports

○ PowerPoint presentations
○ Web copy
○ Instant messages
○ Text messages
○ Other

3. **Are there other things you write at work that aren't mentioned in Question 2?**

_____

_____

4. **Have you ever experienced writer's block?**
   ○ Yes   ○ No

5. **What do you find most challenging about writing at work?**
   ○ I would like to write faster.
   ○ I need to be more concise.
   ○ I have trouble expressing what I really mean.
   ○ I have concerns about correct grammar and punctuation.
   ○ I'd like my writing to be more compelling.
   ○ I have trouble getting started.
   ○ I struggle with writing introductions and openings.
   ○ Other

6. **Now think about your colleagues' writing. Where do you think they could use help with their writing?**

_____

_____

7. **Have you ever used a writing book to improve your writing at work?**
   ○ Yes   ○ No

8. **Would you find a concise, well-organized business writing book helpful?**

   ○ Yes   ○ No   ○ Maybe

9. **Do you think your organization would be interested in purchasing copies of a concise, well-organized business writing book?**

   ○ Yes   ○ No   ○ Maybe

10. **Are there any other thoughts you'd like to share about writing at work?**

   _____

   _____

Appendix B:
List of Common Prepositions

A preposition is a part of speech defined as "a word or group of words that is used with a noun, pronoun, or noun phrase to show direction, location, or time, or to introduce an object." Prepositions introduce prepositional phrases.* For a discussion of prepositional phrases in action, see Step 4 (page 47).

aboard	beneath	for
about	beside	from
above	besides	in
across	between	inside
after	beyond	into
against	but	like
along	by	minus
amid	concerning	near
among	considering	of
anti	despite	off
around	down	on
as	during	onto
at	except	opposite
before	excepting	outside
behind	excluding	over
below	following	past

* *Webster's Ninth New Collegiate Dictionary* (Springfield, Mass., 1983).

per	through	up
plus	to	upon
regarding	toward	versus
round	under	via
save	underneath	with
since	unlike	within
than	until	without

Contributors

Anita Campbell is the founder, CEO, and publisher of *Small Business Trends* (smallbiztrends.com) and its associated online publications, communities, and newsletters. Campbell's expertise has been noted and her opinion quoted in the *Wall Street Journal, New York Times,* and countless other media outlets. She writes one thousand words a day.

Joel Comm is a *New York Times* best-selling author, professional keynote speaker, social media marketing strategist, live video expert, technologist, brand influencer, and futurist. With over two decades of experience in harnessing the power of the web, publishing, social media, and mobile applications to expand, reach, and engage in active relationship marketing, Comm is a sought-after public speaker who leaves his audiences inspired, entertained, and armed with strategic tools with which to create highly effective new media campaigns. His website is joelcomm.com.

Robert C. Daugherty is the executive dean of the Forbes School of Business and Technology. His research areas include leadership, economics, and investment decision-making. Daugherty advises private equity firms, venture capitalists, and corporate business development groups on strategy, governance, and innovation. He has served as a principal, partner, and adviser to a number of funds focused on high-growth and knowledge-based industries. Previously, Daugherty served as the CEO of the Jack Welch Management Institute. He holds degrees from Harvard, Columbia, and the University of Cambridge.

Rachel Christmas Derrick is an editor and award-winning writer who has written six books, several chapters of books, and more than two hundred articles on health, social justice, travel, and other subjects; these were published in the *New York Times, Washington Post, Boston Globe, Los Angeles Times, Miami Herald, Newsweek, Essence, Travel + Leisure, National Geographic Traveler,* and *Islands,* among other periodicals.

She is currently director of communication and fund-raising at the Urban Homesteading Assistance Board, a nonprofit specializing in helping low- to moderate-income New York City residents transform their distressed apartment buildings into strong, self-run affordable housing co-ops. Her previous positions include senior writer at the Rockefeller Foundation and deputy director of communications for University Development and Alumni Relations at Columbia University.

Anita Gupta is head of global media relations and regional head of corporate communications and responsibility, Americas at Deutsche Post DHL Group. She leads the global positioning of Deutsche Post DHL, with its diverse products and services and a base of 450,000 employees in 220 countries. Prior to accepting this assignment, she served the firm in a variety of corporate communications roles globally. Before joining Deutsche Post DHL Group in 2007, she served in several senior risk and communications roles at Citigroup and Citigroup International in New York and Mumbai.

Rich Karlgaard is the publisher and futurist of Forbes Media and a twenty-six-year Forbes employee. His writing is known for its keen assessment of technology, economic, business, and leadership issues.

Karlgaard's 2014 book on innovation culture, *The Soft Edge: Where Great Companies Find Lasting Success,* made the lists of top business books of 2014 for *Inc., *Time.com, 800-CEO-READ, and the *Huffington Post*. His 2015 book, *Team Genius: The New Science of High-Performing*

Organizations, cowritten with Michael S. Malone, was praised by Satya Nadella, CEO of Microsoft. Karlgaard's next book, called *Late Bloomers: The Power of Patience in a World Obsessed with Early Achievement,* will be published by Crown Business in March 2019.

Karlgaard holds a BA in political science from Stanford University. He and his family live in Silicon Valley.

Rieva Lesonsky is a cofounder and the CEO of GrowBiz Media, a custom content-creation company focusing on small businesses and entrepreneurship, and a co-owner of the blog *SmallBizDaily*. A nationally known speaker, best-selling author, and authority on entrepreneurship, Lesonsky has been covering America's entrepreneurs for more than thirty years. Previously, Lesonsky was the longtime editorial director of *Entrepreneur* magazine.

Patty Malenfant is a human resources leader for a Fortune 500 hospitality company in the Washington, D.C., metropolitan area. As a valued business partner with over twenty-five years of experience, she provides expertise in strategic leadership consultation, management coaching, talent acquisition, career development, and organizational development. She has taken key roles in implementing initiatives for leadership talent assessments, performance management, and diversity. Patty enjoys facilitating training and team-building activities to equip leaders with new skills and improve the work environment. Her creative approach to developing and mentoring new team members fosters their career success and job retention.

Barry Moltz gets business owners growing again by unlocking their long-forgotten potential. With decades of entrepreneurial experience in his own business ventures, as well as consulting with countless other entrepreneurs, Barry applies strategic steps to facilitate changes. Barry is the author of five books, including *How to Get Unstuck: 25 Ways to Get Your Business Growing Again* (Motivational Press, 2014).

Jerry Reece has forty-six years of real estate brokerage experience, most recently as chairman emeritus of ReeceNichols, a Berkshire Hathaway affiliate. In 1987, he purchased the residential real estate division of Kroh Brothers and renamed it J. D. Reece Realtors. In 2001, he sold the company to HomeServices of America, a Berkshire Hathaway affiliate. Reece & Nichols was formed in January 2002 with the merger of J. D. Reece Realtors and J. C. Nichols Residential Real Estate. Reece served as the CEO of the enterprise until July 2013. In 2014, Reece & Nichols took it a step further and removed the ampersand from its name. As Reece-Nichols, the name no longer conveys two companies; instead, it speaks of one united brand, its employees standing together as the leader in real estate. Today, ReeceNichols is the market share leader in Kansas City's real estate market. In 2017, Jerry was recognized by Ingram as one of the 250 Most Powerful Business Leaders in Kansas City.

Reece is a graduate of the University of Oregon, with a bachelor of science in finance. He is a Vietnam veteran and a retired colonel in the U.S. Marine Corps Forces Reserve.

Dominique Schurman is the CEO of Schurman Retail Group, whose brands include Papyrus, Marcel Schurman, Paper Destiny, Niquea.D, Carlton Cards, and Clintons. Schurman became CEO in 1992 when her father retired, and she has since increased the number of Papyrus shops from thirty-seven to more than two hundred, in locations throughout North America. Through the acquisition of the Carlton Cards and American Greetings retail stores in 2009, Schurman built the company into a retail powerhouse with more than three hundred stores. Her passion for excellence in product design, product quality, and customer service has helped transform the company from a small niche player into an international collection of retail brands, meeting the needs of both the high-end and the value-oriented consumer.

Steve Strauss is often called "the country's leading small business expert." The senior *USA Today* small business columnist and a best-selling author, Strauss recently updated his all-purpose guide *The Small*

Business Bible, producing a comprehensive third edition. A lawyer, author, and public speaker, Strauss regularly speaks around the world about small business strategies and global trends in business, and he sits on the board of the World Entrepreneurship Forum. Strauss has been seen on ABC, CNN, CNBC, MSNBC, and *The O'Reilly Factor,* among other venues. His company, the Strauss Group, creates cutting-edge business content for everyone from Fortune 100 companies to small chambers of commerce. Strauss's new website for the self-employed is TheSelfEmployed.com.

Sydney Strauss is a writer based in the Pacific Northwest. She is especially passionate about studying language in order to better understand the human condition within a modern, twenty-first-century setting. She received her BA from Seattle University and is eager to continue her higher education in the coming years.

Rosanne J. Thomas is the founder and president of Protocol Advisors, Inc., of Boston, Massachusetts, and the author of *Excuse Me: The Survival Guide to Modern Business Etiquette* (AMACOM, 2017).

Thomas is a certified etiquette and protocol consultant. She believes that "professional presence" is for everyone and that it is never too soon or too late to reap the real benefits enhanced "professional presence" provides. Thomas travels the country presenting training programs designed to instill confidence and help professionals achieve their personal goals for success.

Recognized as an expert in her field, Thomas makes frequent appearances on television and radio shows and in print. She was featured in the *Boston Globe*'s article "Miss Manners on Wall Street" and has contributed to the WCVB TV show *Chronicle,* as well as to WHDH, WBZ, and FOX television programs. Additionally, she has been interviewed on *CBS This Morning,* MTV, and National Public Radio and has been featured in articles in the *Wall Street Journal, Newsweek,* and *Entrepreneur* magazine. Thomas's professional background also includes eleven years with the internationally renowned luxury retailer Tiffany & Co.

Index

About the Author

Laura Brown, **PhD**, is the author of *How to Write Anything: A Complete Guide* (W. W. Norton, 2014), an Amazon No. 1 best seller in the business communications category. Her business writing training and coaching clients have included AOL Time Warner, Citigroup, DHL, Dun & Bradstreet, the Ford Foundation, Hay Group, Morgan Stanley Smith Barney, Prudential, TMP Worldwide, and Warburg Pincus, among others.

Laura taught business and technical writing at Iona College for ten years, and she taught composition at Columbia University for five. She designed two core courses for Columbia's master's program in strategic communication. Laura has an extensive background in digital learning design. In 1999, she collaborated with e-learning pioneer Roger Schank and Columbia University on a series of web-based business writing courses. She has developed a variety of corporate training programs with online learning companies Cognitive Arts, KLi Learning Corporation, and Socratic Arts.

As a writer, Laura has provided a variety of marketing and other writing services—including web content, business cases, white papers, and promotional materials—for clients like Booz Allen Hamilton, Columbia Business School, Corning Incorporated, and Deloitte. She served for three years as English communication adviser for the Wharton School's Global Chinese Business Initiative, where she oversaw the writing of international correspondence, promotional literature, and a series of case studies.

Laura is the coauthor of *Build Your Own Garage: Blueprints and Tools to Unleash Your Company's Hidden Creativity* (Free Press, 2001) with Professor Bernd H. Schmitt of Columbia Business School. She has ghostwritten nearly a dozen books, including *Inside Chinese Business: A Guide for Managers Worldwide* (Harvard Business School Press, 2001) by Professor Ming-Jer Chen and *Experiential Marketing: How to Get Customers to Sense, Feel, Think, Act, and Relate to Your Company and Brands* (Free Press, 1999) by Bernd H. Schmitt (in this best-selling marketing book, "Laura Brown" also appears as a mystery character . . .).

Laura Brown was born in California and received a BA in English from UCLA. She holds an MA in drama from the University of London and a PhD in English and comparative literature from Columbia University. She lives in New York City.

You can reach Laura via www.howtowriteanything.com and www.laurabrowncommunications.com.